PENGUIN 🐧 LIBERTY

HAMILTON

Corey Brettschneider is a professor of political science at Brown University, where he teaches constitutional law and politics, as well as a visiting professor of law at Fordham University School of Law. He has also been a visiting professor at Harvard Law School and the University of Chicago Law School. His writing has appeared in *The New York Times*, *Politico*, and *The Washington Post*. He is the author of *The Oath and the Office: A Guide to the Constitution for Future Presidents*, two books about constitutional law and civil liberties, and numerous articles published in academic journals and law reviews. His constitutional law casebook is widely used in classrooms throughout the United States. Brettschneider holds a PhD in politics from Princeton University and a JD from Stanford Law School.

HAMILTON

Selected Writings

EDITED WITH AN INTRODUCTION BY
Corey Brettschneider

SERIES EDITOR
Corey Brettschneider

PENGUIN BOOKS

PENGUIN BOOKS
An imprint of Penguin Random House LLC
penguinrandomhouse.com

Series introduction copyright © 2020 by Corey Brettschneider
Volume introduction and selection copyright © 2023 by Corey
Brettschneider

LIBRARY OF CONGRESS CATALOGING-IN-PUBLICATION DATA
Names: Hamilton, Alexander, 1757-1804, author |
Brettschneider, Corey Lang, editor.
Title: Hamilton : selected writings / edited with an introduction
by Corey Brettschneider.
Description: [New York] : Penguin Books, [2023] |
Series: Penguin liberty | Includes bibliographical references.
Identifiers: LCCN 2022059165 (print) | LCCN 2022059166 (ebook) |
ISBN 9780143135128 (paperback) | ISBN 9780525506805 (ebook)
Subjects: LCSH: Hamilton, Alexander, 1757-1804—Sources. |
United States—Politics and government—To 1775—Sources. |
United States—Politics and government—1775-1783—Sources. |
United States—Politics and government—1783-1809—Sources. |
Statesmen—United States.
Classification: LCC E302.H22 2023 (print) |
LCC E302.H22 (ebook)| DDC 973.4092—dc23/eng/20230203
LC record available at https://lccn.loc.gov/2022059165
LC ebook record available at https://lccn.loc.gov/2022059166

Printed in the United States of America
1st Printing

Set in Adobe Caslon
Designed by Daniel Lagin

Contents

Series Introduction by Corey Brettschneider   ix

Introduction by Corey Brettschneider   xxv

A Note on the Text   xxxiii

HAMILTON

Part I: IS PROTEST DISLOYALTY?: A PREREVOLUTIONARY DEBATE

Free Thoughts on the Proceedings of the Continental Congress at Philadelphia, by Samuel Seabury (1774)   3

A Full Vindication of the Measures of the Congress, by Alexander Hamilton (1774)   13

The Farmer Refuted, by Alexander Hamilton (1775)   29

Part II: IS THE CONSTITUTION TYRANNICAL?: THE DEBATE OVER RATIFICATION

HAMILTON V. BRUTUS (CONSTITUTION RATIFICATION)

Brutus No. 1 (1787)   45

The Federalist No. 9, by Alexander Hamilton (1787)   51

Brutus No. 2 (1787)   56

The Federalist No. 84, by
Alexander Hamilton (1788)   64

HAMILTON V. GEORGE MASON
(PARDONING POWERS)

Debate In Virginia Ratifying Convention (1788)   71

The Federalist No. 69, by
Alexander Hamilton (1788)   73

Part III: DOES A STRONG GOVERNMENT USURP FREEDOM?: THE DEBATES OVER THE BANK OF THE UNITED STATES AND THE WAR POWERS

HAMILTON V. JAMES MADISON AND THOMAS
JEFFERSON (BANK OF THE UNITED STATES)

"The Bank Bill," by James Madison (1791)   81

"Jefferson's Opinion on the Constitutionality of
a National Bank" (1791)   92

"Hamilton's Opinion as to the Constitutionality of
a National Bank" (1791)   100

HAMILTON V. JAMES MADISON
(WAR POWERS)

The Proclamation of Neutrality of 1793, by
George Washington   113

THE PACIFICUS-HELVIDIUS DEBATE

Pacificus No. 1, by Alexander Hamilton (1793)   115

Helvidius No. 1, by James Madison (1793)   120

Helvidius No. 2, by James Madison (1793)   123

Part IV: PERSONALITY OR POLITICS?: ALEXANDER HAMILTON'S INSULTS

"Special Session Message to Congress (XYZ Affair)," by John Adams (1797)   127

"Concerning the Public Conduct and Character of John Adams, Esq.," by Alexander Hamilton (1800)   138

Letter to Aaron Burr Denying the Accusations, by Alexander Hamilton (1804)   153

Letter to Alexander Hamilton on Alleged Personal Insults, by Aaron Burr (1804)   156

On Dueling, by Alexander Hamilton (1804)   158

Acknowledgments   163
Unabridged Source Materials   165

Series Introduction

On November 9, 1989, the Berlin Wall fell. Two years later, in December 1991, the Soviet Union collapsed. These events, markers of the end of the Cold War, were seen by many as the final triumphant victory of democracy over authoritarianism and communism. Political scientist Francis Fukuyama famously declared the era to be the "end of history," suggesting that Western-style liberalism was the ultimate form of human ideology. There was a strong consensus—at least in the West—that liberal freedoms were necessary in any society.

But since then, that consensus has been shaken. In the twenty-first century, democracies have crumbled across the globe, with authoritarian leaders grabbing power and eroding traditional rights protections. Examples abound. Mexico and the Philippines embarked on extrajudicial drug wars; Nicolás Maduro's regime brought a state of near-famine to Venezuela; Poland's Law and Justice Party functionally turned parts of the media into its propaganda arm. In countless other countries, leaders have impinged on citizens' freedom. Even the United States—where liberal freedoms have often been taken for granted—has faced powerful movements and leaders who have disputed the legitimacy of the very rights that underpin our democracy.

Yet in the United States, calls to restrict rights have always run up against a powerful adversary, one that dates back to the country's founding: the Constitution of the United States. This Penguin Liberty series is designed to explore the Constitution's protections, illuminating how its text and values can help us as modern citizens to reflect on the meaning of liberty and understand how to defend it. With rights-based democracy under attack from all angles, it is crucial to engage in ongoing discussion about the meaning of liberty, its limits, and its role in the modern world.

Certainly, the ideal of liberty has been present in America since the dawn of the American Revolution, when Patrick Henry reportedly declared, "Give me liberty, or give me death!" In 1776, the Declaration of Independence proclaimed liberty an "unalienable Right"—along with "Life" and the "pursuit of Happiness"—enshrining it as a central American aspiration.

These statements, however, are only a start in thinking about liberty. Mistakenly, they seem to suggest that liberty is absolute, never limited. But in this series, we will see that idea continually challenged. Various liberties sometimes conflict, and we must deliberate among them. Importantly, the liberty to be free from government intervention, or what the British philosopher Isaiah Berlin called "negative liberty," must sometimes be balanced against our liberty as a democratic people to govern in the general interest, an idea he called "positive liberty." Thus, the series will also emphasize the importance of liberty not only in terms of freedom from government intervention but also as self-government, the freedom of all of us collectively to decide on our own destinies.

Ratified in 1788, the Constitution was an attempt to codify the high ideal of liberty as self-government. Through intense debate at the Constitutional Convention, a document was forged that limited government power and gave people a say in how they were to be governed. Its goal was to "secure the Blessings of Liberty to ourselves and our Posterity." Still, many Americans were not convinced the Constitution went far enough in protecting their individual freedom from government coercion—what Berlin would call "negative liberty." Although the push for a Bill of Rights failed at the Constitutional Convention, the First Congress ratified one in 1791. These first ten amendments to the Constitution focused largely on securing individual liberties.

Just over 4,500 words long when originally passed, the U.S. Constitution is the shortest written governing charter of any major democracy. Its brevity belies its impact. Ours is the world's longest surviving written constitution. Some scholars estimate that, at one time, as many as 160 other nations based their constitution at least in part on the U.S. Constitution. The United Nations Universal Declaration of Human Rights from 1948 overlaps significantly with provisions of our Bill of Rights. Individual freedoms that our Constitution champions inspire peoples across the globe.

Of course, the original Constitution protected liberty for only a restricted few. As written in 1787, the Constitution did not explicitly outlaw racialized chattel slavery. Almost 700,000 Black people were enslaved in the United States at the time of its founding, a fact that the Constitution did nothing to change and tacitly allowed. Article I prohibited Congress from outlawing the international slave trade until 1808, and the three-fifths clause cemented Southern white political power by having enslaved people count toward political representation without allowing them to vote.

Not all the framers wanted the Constitution to be tainted by slavery. James Madison and Alexander Hamilton, for example, thought slavery morally wrong. But they were willing to compromise this conviction in order for Southern states to ratify the document they so cherished. Thus was born America's original sin, a legally sanctioned system of racial oppression that persisted formally until the Civil War. Only after more than an estimated 600,000 Americans gave their lives in that bloody conflict was the Constitution amended to outlaw slavery, guarantee "equal protection of the laws," and establish that race could deny no citizen access to the franchise.

Enslaved Americans were not the only ones left out of the original Constitution's promise of liberty. Women were guaranteed no formal rights under the Constitution, and they were deprived of equal political status until 1920, when suffragists finally succeeded in amending the Constitution to guarantee women the vote. In the Founding Era, the vote in many states was restricted mainly to white male property owners.

These significant failures are reasons to criticize the Constitution. But they should not lead anyone to discount it altogether. First, the Constitution has demonstrated a remarkable resilience and capacity for change. In each of the cases described above, the Constitution was later amended to attempt to rectify the wrong and expand citizens' rights. Second, and perhaps more important, the Constitution's deepest values have often inspired and strengthened the hand of those seeking justice. That's why Frederick Douglass, himself a former enslaved person, became an ardent supporter of the Constitution, even before the passage of the post–Civil War amendments that ended slavery and provided equal rights. In his Fourth of July oration in 1852, he praised the Constitution as a "glorious liberty document" but added a crucial caveat: it protected liberty only when it was "interpreted as it ought to be interpreted." Douglass believed that while many saw the Constitution as a proslavery document, its text and values supported broad protections for freedom and equality.

Douglass's point, though delivered more than 150 years

ago, inspires this Penguin Liberty series. The Constitution is not a static document. Nor is it just a set of provisions on paper. The Constitution is a legal document containing specific rules, but it also gives voice to a broader public morality that transcends any one rule.

What exactly that public morality stands for has always been up for debate and interpretation. Today, after the passage of the post–Civil War amendments, the Constitution takes a clear stand against racial subordination. But there are still many other vital questions of liberty on which the Constitution offers guidance without dictating one definite answer. Through the processes of interpretation, amendment, and debate, the Constitution's guarantees of liberty have, over time, become more fully realized.

In these volumes, we will look to the Constitution's text and values, as well as to American history and some of its most important thinkers, to discover the best explanations of our constitutional ideals of liberty. Though imperfect, the Constitution can be the country's guiding light in dark times, illuminating a path to the recovery of liberty. My hope is that these volumes offer readers the chance to hear the strongest defenses of constitutional ideals, gaining new (or renewed) appreciation for values that have long sustained the nation.

No single fixed or perfectly clear meaning of the Constitution will emerge from this series. Constitutional statements of liberty are often brief, open to multiple interpretations. Competing values within the document raise difficult questions, such as how to balance freedom and equality, or privacy and security. I hope that as you learn from the important texts in these volumes, you undertake a critical examination of what liberty means to you—and how the Constitution should be interpreted to protect it. Though the popular understanding may be that the Supreme Court is the final arbiter of the

Constitution, constitutional liberty is best protected when not just every branch of government but also every citizen is engaged in constitutional interpretation. Questions of liberty affect both our daily lives and our country's values, from what we can say to whom we can marry, how society views us to how we determine our leaders. It is Americans' great privilege that we live under a Constitution that both protects our liberty and allows us to debate what that liberty should be.

The central features of constitutional liberty are freedom and equality, values that are often in tension. One of the Constitution's most important declarations of freedom comes in the First Amendment, which provides that "Congress shall make no law respecting an establishment of religion, or prohibiting the free exercise thereof; or abridging the freedom of speech, or of the press; or the right of the people peaceably to assemble, and to petition the Government for a redress of grievances." And one of its most important declarations of equality comes in the Fourteenth Amendment, which reads in part, "no State shall . . . deny to any person within its jurisdiction the equal protection of the laws." These Penguin Liberty volumes look in depth at these conceptions of liberty while also exploring what mechanisms the Constitution has to protect its guarantees of liberty.

Freedom of speech provides a good place to begin to explore the Constitution's idea of liberty. It is a value that enables both the protection of liberty and the right of citizens to debate its meaning. Textually, the constitutional guarantee that Congress cannot limit free speech might read as though it is absolute. Yet for much of U.S. history, free speech protections were minimal. In 1798, President John Adams signed the Sedition Act, essentially making it a crime to criticize the president or the U.S. government. During the Civil War, President Abraham Lincoln had some dissidents and newspapers silenced. In 1919, a moment came that seemed to protect free speech, when Justice Oliver Wendell Holmes wrote in *Schenck v. United States* that speech could be limited only when it posed a "clear and present danger." But, in fact, this ruling did little to protect free speech, as the Court repeatedly interpreted danger so broadly that minority viewpoints, especially leftist viewpoints, were often seen as imprisonable.

Today, however, U.S. free speech protections are the most expansive in the world. All viewpoints are allowed to be expressed, except for direct threats and incitements to violence. Even many forms of hate speech and opinions attacking democracy itself—types of speech that would be illegal in other countries—are generally permitted here, in the name of free expression. The Court's governing standard is annunciated in *Brandenburg v. Ohio*, which protects vast amounts of speech as long as that speech does not incite "imminent lawless action." How did we get from the Sedition Act to here?

Two thinkers have played an outsize role: John Stuart Mill and Alexander Meiklejohn. Mill's 1859 classic, *On Liberty*, is an ode to the idea that both liberty and truth will thrive in an open exchange of ideas, where all opinions are allowed to be challenged. In this "marketplace of ideas," as Mill's idea has often come to be called, the truth stays vibrant instead of decaying or descending into dogma. Mill's idea explains the virtue of free speech and the importance of a book series about liberty: Challenging accepted ideas about what liberty is helps bring the best ideas to light. Meiklejohn's theory focuses more on the connection between free speech and democracy. To him, the value of free speech is as much for the listeners as it is for the speakers. In a democracy, only when citizens hear all ideas can they come to informed conclusions about how society should be governed. And only informed citizens can fully exercise other democratic rights besides speech, like the right to vote. Meiklejohn's insistence that democratic citizens need a broad exposure to ideas of liberty inspires this series.

Freedom of religion is another central constitutional value that allows citizens the liberty to be who they are and believe what they wish. It is enshrined in the First Amendment, where the Establishment Clause prevents government endorsement of a religion and the Free Exercise Clause gives citizens the freedom to practice their religion. Though these two religion clauses are widely embraced now, they were radically new at the time of the nation's founding. Among the first European settlers in America were the Puritans, members of a group of English Protestants who were persecuted for their religion in their native Britain. But colonial America did not immediately and totally embrace religious toleration. The Church of England still held great sway in the South during the colonial era, and many states had official religions—even after the Constitution forbade a national religion. At the time the Constitution was ratified, secular government was a rarity.

But religious tolerance was eventually enshrined into the U.S. Constitution, thanks in large part to the influence of two thinkers. British philosopher John Locke opposed systems of theocracy. He saw how government-imposed religious beliefs stifled the freedom of minority believers and imposed religious dogma on unwilling societies. In the United States, James Madison built on Locke's ideas when he drafted the First Amendment. The Free Exercise Clause protected the personal freedom to worship, acknowledging the importance of religious practice among Americans. But on Madison's understanding, the Establishment Clause ensured against theocratic imposition of religion by government. Doing so respected the equality of citizens by refusing to allow the government to favor some people's religious beliefs over others.

A more explicit defense of equality comes from the Equal Protection Clause of the Fourteenth Amendment. But as our volume on the Supreme Court shows, the Constitution has not always been interpreted to promote equality. Before the Civil War, African Americans had few, if any, formal rights. Millions of African American people were enslaved, and so-called congressional compromises maintained racial subordination long after the importation of slaves was banned in 1808. A burgeoning abolitionist movement gained moral momentum in the North, though the institution of slavery persisted. Liberty was a myth for enslaved people, who were unable to move freely, form organizations, earn wages, or participate in politics.

Still, the Supreme Court, the supposed protector of liberty, for decades failed to guarantee it for African Americans. And in its most notorious ruling it revealed the deep-seated prejudices that had helped to perpetuate slavery. Chief Justice Roger Taney wrote in the 1857 decision in *Dred Scott v. Sandford* that African Americans were not citizens of the United States and "had no rights which the white man was bound to respect." Taney's words were one spark for the Civil War, which, once won by the Union, led to the passage of the Thirteenth, Fourteenth, and Fifteenth Amendments. By ending slavery, granting citizenship and mandating equal legal protection, and outlawing racial discrimination in voting, these Reconstruction Amendments sought to reverse Taney's heinous opinion and provide a platform for advancing real equality.

History unfortunately shows us, however, that legal equality did not translate into real equality for African Americans.

Soon after Reconstruction, the Court eviscerated the Fourteenth Amendment's scope, then ruled in 1896 in *Plessy v. Ferguson* that racial segregation was constitutional if the separate facilities were deemed equal. This paved the way for the legally sanctioned institution of Jim Crow segregation, which relegated African Americans to second-class citizenship, denying them meaningful social, legal, and political equality. Finally, facing immense pressure from civil rights advocates including W. E. B. Du Bois and A. Philip Randolph, as well as the powerful legal reasoning of NAACP lawyer Thurgood Marshall, the Court gave the Equal Protection Clause teeth, culminating in the landmark 1954 *Brown v. Board of Education* decision, which declared that separate is "inherently unequal." Even after that newfound defense of constitutional equality, however, racial inequality has persisted, with the Court and country debating the meaning of liberty and equal protection in issues as varied as affirmative action and racial gerrymandering.

While the Fourteenth Amendment was originally passed with a specific intention to end racial discrimination, its language is general: "No State shall . . . deny to any person within its jurisdiction the equal protection of the laws." Over time, that generality has allowed civil rights advocates to expand the meaning of equality to include other groups facing discrimination. One significant example is the fight for gender equality.

Women had been left out of the Constitution; masculine pronouns pepper the original document, and women are not mentioned. In an 1807 letter to Albert Gallatin, Thomas Jefferson—the person who had penned the Declaration of Independence—wrote that "the appointment of a woman to office is an innovation for which the public is not prepared, nor am I." Liberty was a myth for many women, who were supposed to do little outside the home, had limited rights to property, were often made to be financially dependent on their husbands, and faced immense barriers to political participation.

Nevertheless, women refused to be shut out of politics. Many were influential in the burgeoning temperance and abolition movements of the nineteenth century. In 1848, Elizabeth Cady Stanton wrote the Declaration of Sentiments, amending the Declaration of Independence to include women. Still, suffragists were left out when the Fifteenth Amendment banned voting discrimination based on race—but not on gender. Only after Alice Paul and others led massive protests would the freedom to vote be constitutionally guaranteed for women through the Nineteenth Amendment.

Voting secured one key democratic liberty, but women were still denied the full protection of legal equality. They faced discrimination in the workplace, laws based on sexist stereotypes, and a lack of reproductive autonomy. That's where our volume on Supreme Court justice Ruth Bader Ginsburg begins. Now a feminist icon from her opinions on the Court, Justice Ginsburg earlier served as a litigator with the ACLU, leading their Women's Rights Project, where she helped to convince the Court to consider gender as a protected class under the Fourteenth Amendment. As a justice, she continued her pioneering work to deliver real gender equality, knowing that women would never enjoy the full scope of constitutional liberty unless they held the same legal status as men.

Ginsburg's work underscores how the meaning of constitutional liberty has expanded over time. While the Declaration of Independence did explicitly reference equality, the Bill of Rights did not. Then, with the Reconstruction Amendments, especially the Equal Protection Clause, the Constitution was imbued with a new commitment to equality. Now the document affirmed that democratic societies must protect both negative liberties for citizens to act freely and positive liberties for all to be treated as equal democratic citizens. Never has this tension between freedom and equality been perfectly resolved, but the story of our Constitution is that it has often inspired progress toward realizing liberty for more Americans.

Progress has been possible not just because of an abstract constitutional commitment to liberty but also due to formal mechanisms that help us to guarantee it. Impeachment is the Constitution's most famous—and most explosive—way to do so. With the abuses of monarchy in mind, the framers needed a way to thwart tyranny and limit concentrated power. Borrowing in language and spirit from the British, who created a system of impeachment to check the power of the king, they wrote this clause into the Constitution: "The President . . . shall be removed from Office on Impeachment for, and Conviction of, Treason, Bribery, or other high Crimes and Misdemeanors."

Early drafts suggested grounds for impeachment should be just "treason or bribery." But George Mason and other delegates objected, wanting impeachable offenses to include broader abuses of power, not just criminal actions. Though Mason's original suggestion of "maladministration" was rejected, the ultimate language of "high Crimes and Misdemeanors" made it possible to pursue impeachment against leaders who threatened the Constitution's deeper values. Impeachment would stand as the ultimate check on officials who overstep their constitutional authority.

The House has formally impeached twenty officials throughout American history, and many more have faced some kind of impeachment inquiry. Most of those accused have been federal judges. Just five impeachment proceedings have reached the presidency, the highest echelon of American government. Andrew Johnson and Bill Clinton were each formally impeached once and Donald Trump was formally impeached twice, though none of these presidents were convicted and removed from office. Richard Nixon resigned after the House Judiciary Committee voted to impeach, before the full House vote could take place. Most of these impeachment proceedings had a background context in which a president was thought to have violated fundamental constitutional liberties—even if that violation was not always the primary component of the impeachment hearings themselves.

For Johnson, although his impeachment focused on the Tenure of Office Act, an underlying issue was his violation of the liberty of newly freed African Americans to live in society as equals. For Nixon, the impeachment inquiry focused on the Watergate break-in and cover-up, which threatened the liberty of voters to have fair elections to hold their presidents criminally accountable. For Clinton, who was accused of perjury and obstruction of justice related to a sexual affair with a White House intern, critics argued that his flouting of criminal laws threatened the standard of equal justice under law—a standard necessary for democratic self-government. For Trump, the impeachment articles in his first trial accused him of soliciting foreign interference as an abuse of power—threatening the liberty of voters to have fair elections; his second impeachment trial accused him of inciting an insurrection to prevent the peaceful transfer of power between administrations, threatening that previously uninterrupted hallmark of American democracy. Often, legalistic questions of criminal wrongdoing dominated these impeachment discussions, but concerns about violations of constitutional liberty were frequently present in the background.

While impeachment is an important remedy for presidential abuse of liberty, liberty lives best when it is respected before crises arise. To do so requires that liberty not be relegated to an idea just for the purview of courts; rather, citizens and officials should engage in discussions about the meaning of liberty, reaffirming its centrality in everyday life.

There are few people for whom those discussions are better modeled than the now hip-hop famous Alexander Hamilton, a founding father and the nation's first secretary of the treasury. Hamilton was a prolific writer, and in our volumes we'll see him square off against other founders in debates on many major challenges facing the early republic. Against Samuel Seabury, Hamilton rejected the British colonial system and said liberty must come through independence. Against Thomas Jefferson (in an argument now immortalized as a Broadway rap battle), Hamilton advocated for a national bank, believing that a modern, industrial economy was needed to grow the nation. Against James Madison, he pushed for stronger foreign policy powers for the president.

The specifics of Hamilton's debates matter. His ideas shaped American notions of government power, from self-determination to economic growth to international engagement. He was instrumental in ratifying the very Constitution that still protects our liberties today. But just as important as *what* he argued for was *how* he argued for it. Hamilton thought deeply about what liberty meant to him, and he engaged in thoughtful, reasoned discussions with people he disagreed with. He cared both for his own freedoms and for the country's welfare at large.

My goal is for readers of these Penguin Liberty volumes to emulate Hamilton's passion for defending his ideas—even, or especially, if they disagree with him on what liberty means. Everyday citizens are the most important readers of this series—and the most important Americans in the struggle to protect and expand constitutional liberty. Without pressure from the citizenry to uphold constitutional ideals, elected leaders can too easily scrap them. Without citizens vigorously examining the meaning of liberty, its power could be lost. Left untended, the flames of liberty could quietly burn out.

The writings in these Penguin Liberty volumes are intended to give citizens the tools to contest and explore the meaning of liberty so it may be kept alive. None of the selections are simple enough to be summed up in tweets or dismissed with quick insults. They are reasoned, thoughtful attempts to defend constitutional ideals of liberty—or warnings about what can happen when those liberties are disregarded. The Constitution's guarantees of liberty have always been aspirations, not realized accomplishments. Yet if these volumes and other constitutional writings inspire us to bring discussions to dinner tables, classrooms, and workplaces across the country, they will be contributing to making those high ideals more real.

COREY BRETTSCHNEIDER

Introduction

Alexander Hamilton—legendary framer of the Constitution, and subject of an iconic musical and a best-selling biography—had his fair share of enemies during his lifetime. For those who despised him, a prominent charge was that this man, a supposed lover of liberty and democracy, was more devoted to monarchy. Famously, Thomas Jefferson said of Hamilton that he was not only for monarchy, but "for a monarchy bottomed on corruption."* Are the millions of fans who sing Alexander Hamilton's name today actually celebrating an opponent of democratic liberty?

Hamilton's political views and their relationship with democratic liberty are complicated. To understand them requires a deep dive into the relationship between government and freedom. Liberty is commonly defined as freedom from government action. But a close study of Hamilton shows he embraced a more sophisticated idea. Hamilton consistently argued for a strong federal government to avoid chaos. He did not see a robust government standing in opposition to freedom but as a necessary precondition to guarantee it in the first place.

*Thomas Jefferson, "Explanations of the 3. Volumes Bound in Marbled Paper," February 4, 1818, Founders Online, National Archives, https://founders.archives.gov/documents/Jefferson/03-12-02-0343-0002.

Hamilton had very likely studied John Locke and his views about freedom while a student at King's College (now Columbia University). In that philosopher's ideas lie the origin of Hamilton's own approach to politics. Locke distinguishes between "license" and "liberty" in his Second Treatise of Government. By "license," Locke referred to the state of anarchy that would result in nature from the absence of strong government. Without government to bring order, Locke argued, people would be aware of one another's rights but fail badly in protecting them. Therefore, for Locke, an active government is needed to secure "natural rights" and to safeguard fundamental liberties. In other words, anarchy, which results from weak government, is the enemy of liberty. In contrast, strong government is its ally. That philosophy would define Hamilton's many debates over his lifetime.

To see why Hamilton regarded strong government as an aspect of liberty as opposed to license, it is crucial to provide some historical context for his view. Hamilton first came to prominence in the aftermath of the Boston Tea Party, in 1774, when he defended the actions of the First Continental Congress. The assembly, meeting that year in Philadelphia, had resisted calls for outright revolution against the British crown. Instead, the Congress issued a petition to King George III protesting heavy taxation by the British Parliament and new restrictions on self-governance in the colonies. The Anglican bishop Samuel Seabury, writing under the pen name A. W. Farmer, decried the disloyalty of those who attended the Congress. The assembly stopped short of revolution but had shown disloyalty to the crown, as Seabury saw it. In the musical *Hamilton*, Seabury sings that the delegates are courting disaster. The tone of Seabury's real-life pamphlet was much harsher. Seabury argued that being subject to a king was not slavery, but even if it were, it was preferable to subjecting oneself to the decisions of the First Continental Congress. As A. W. Farmer put it, "If I must be enslaved, let it be by a KING at least, and not by a parcel of upstart lawless Committeemen."

Hamilton responded to Seabury's commentary and those that followed in a series of writings. In the essay "The Farmer Refuted," Hamilton gives readers a window into his core ideas about liberty and natural rights. Colonial governments, like all governments, Hamilton argues, exist to defend natural rights. They are responsible for protecting property and enabling wealth creation. If Parliament's restrictions on the colonies only serve to punish them, then these restrictions undermine the very basis by which the colonial government rules, he argues. That Seabury fails to understand this basic point makes it clear the "enmity, you [Seabury] have discovered to the *natural rights* of mankind." At this early point in his career, Hamilton was not yet demanding freedom from British rule. He instead called only for government to serve its purpose in securing property rights.

While Hamilton's first debate saw him defend and define liberty in the context of colonial government, in his next battle he defended a proposed new Constitution. At the Constitutional Convention itself, held in Philadelphia in 1787, delegates originally convened to strengthen the weak Articles of Confederation that had governed the nascent country since the revolution. But soon the Convention took a more radical direction, proposing an entirely new Constitution. Debate ensued about how strong the new federal government should be. Hamilton argued for robust federal power, pushing the view that the document should provide for a strong executive and more power for Congress to tax and spend. Some delegates argued that an overly strong federal government could lead to tyranny and dangerously weaken the power of state governments. After the convention, anti-Federalists argued that the danger of the proposed federal government was so great that the American people should refuse to ratify the Constitution. A series of essays written under the pen name Brutus developed the arguments originally raised at the Convention that the new Constitution eviscerated the role of state governments, which were closer to the people than a national government could be. George Mason, a delegate to the convention from Philadelphia who joined Brutus and the anti-Federalists in attacking the Constitution, particularly emphasized the danger of the proposed office of the presidency. Mason argued that the vast powers of the office left it vulnerable to an occupant who lacked virtue and sought monarchical power. Specifically, a criminally minded president, Mason argued, could use the power to pardon to enable co-conspirators to get away with their crimes.

Hamilton had been a major force in shaping the proposed Constitution and its creation of a strong center of federal power. Now, with Brutus and others on the attack, Hamilton picked up his pen to respond, joining with James Madison and John Jay to write a series of newspaper articles defending the Constitution, collectively known as *The Federalist*. To Brutus's accusation that the Constitution stunted the states' power, Hamilton turned to history, explaining that the new system would avoid the anarchy that marked the "petty republics of Greece and Italy." Brutus had wrongly assumed that strong federal power meant an absence of liberty. What it really meant, Hamilton argued, was a way of pushing back on anarchy, the true threat to liberty. To Mason's argument about the danger of the president's vast powers, Hamilton responded that the power of the proposed office of the president was more limited than those of state governors. In Hamilton's view, tyranny was more likely to arise at the state level than that of the federal government. *The Federalist* repeatedly stressed the need for a strong central government to combat the risk of chaos, a task states could not fulfill on their own. It is government action, Hamilton argued, that protects liberty and the absence of it that invites anarchy. Hamilton won the debate, of course, as the Constitution was ratified. His role in history and the central importance of *The Federalist* to understanding the Constitution was solidified.

After ratification, Hamilton's most significant debates shifted from the threat that the Constitution posed to liberty to disagreements over how to interpret the document to fulfill its promise. But this new phase of American history and the debate that came with it saw Hamilton return to a familiar theme. Strong presidential power did not threaten liberty. It allowed presidents to use their "energy" to secure liberty for the people. Lin-Manuel Miranda famously brought the first of these debates to musical life in *Hamilton* when he portrayed Hamilton in an epic rap battle with Secretary of State Thomas Jefferson. Their argument centered on whether Congress had the power to establish a national bank. Jefferson saw the bank as a Trojan horse for excessive federal power. Hamilton pushed back by pointing to three words of the Constitution's text. Hamilton argued that when the Constitution gave Congress the power to do what was "necessary and proper," it provided a broad grant of power to that body to enact laws that promoted economic well-being. The Constitution was not, as Hamilton's opponents would argue, a document that largely constrained federal power. The bank was needed to stave off the economic insecurity that invited instability. Hamilton thus prefigured later presidents, like Franklin Roosevelt, who would argue that an active federal role in the economy was necessary to actively secure freedom from "want" and "fear."

Another similar debate, this time with James Madison, also centered on federal power. The controversy began on April 22, 1793, when President George Washington declared the United States neutral in the war between France and England. Madison favored France in the conflict, but Hamilton sought not to alienate England. Even as they focused on United States foreign policy, the meaning of liberty was an underlying source of tension between the two men. Hamilton and Madison had worked together, both contributing to the Federalist Papers in defense of the Constitution. Now, dramatically, they were in fierce opposition. In defending the president's constitutional power to declare neutrality, Hamilton was bringing to international politics what he had long argued for in domestic politics: To protect freedom, a president needed strength, and that was particularly true during emergencies in which the nation might be led into war. Madison argued the opposite: In seizing more power than the Constitution gave him, Washington veered the fledgling republic back toward monarchy. British kings enjoyed the power to initiate war, a power Madison noted was explicitly denied to American presidents to prevent the risk of monarchy.

Although Hamilton faced criticism throughout his life that he aggrandized the presidency and that his ideas threatened liberty in the United States, he was willing to criticize presidents he thought went too far. John Adams, like Hamilton, was a fellow founder of the Federalist Party. During Adams's administration, however, Hamilton thought this president was failing badly, falling prey to his own egotistical tendencies. His criticism of Adams shows Hamilton using his own freedom to confront a sitting president. It's a sobering moment—a defender of vast federal power, seeing how an ill-tempered president, far from acting with the virtuous energy

Hamilton saw in Washington, was instead ruling based on his worst vices.

The United States is still grappling with the debates that defined Hamilton's life. His view of federal power to enact laws "necessary and proper" to carry out the Constitution is under attack by Supreme Court justices who want to curb federal power in areas like health care and environmental protection. Debates over the extent and danger of the president's pardon power were reignited during the Trump era, as the president pardoned Roger Stone, a close ally. And the debates over the president's war powers reemerged among members of Congress as President Joe Biden weighed different measures to support Ukraine's efforts to defend itself against Russian invasion. To fully understand these pressing contemporary issues, readers should start where these debates began—with Hamilton's debates over liberty. Whether you emerge from this volume sympathetic to Hamilton's views or completely at odds with them, you will be better prepared to see how today's political conflicts are rooted in the historical debates in which Hamilton played a central role.

COREY BRETTSCHNEIDER

A Note on the Text

All the works in this volume are excerpted from full original source documents. Spelling and punctuation are kept as in the original. Footnotes have been eliminated from the text without marking. All works can be found within the Unabridged Source Materials section in this book.

HAMILTON

Part I

IS PROTEST DISLOYALTY?

———— ☆ ————

A Prerevolutionary Debate

After the First Continental Congress met in 1774 to criticize aspects of British rule, some loyalists like Anglican bishop Samuel Seabury spoke out against this perceived disloyalty. Hamilton pushed back. In his debate with Seabury, Hamilton seems to be drawing heavily from the natural rights theory of English philosopher John Locke. These essays see Hamilton at his most philosophical, returning repeatedly to the question of what makes governments legitimate at their foundation. Drawing on Locke, Hamilton argues the protection of natural rights is the central requirement of government. And, Locke adds, to have the privilege of protecting those rights government must also retain the consent of the governed, which tyrannical parliamentary action threatens to undermine. The historical details here are important—much of the debate concerns specific actions the British government took that colonists saw as oppressive. But the core of the debate extends beyond the historical moment, illustrating Hamilton's complex idea of the purposes of government and the nature of political liberty.

Free Thoughts on the Proceedings of the Continental Congress at Philadelphia, by Samuel Seabury (1774)

My Friends and Countrymen,

PERMIT me to address you upon a subject, which, next to your eternal welfare in a future world, demands your most serious and dispassionate consideration. The American Colonies are unhappily involved in a scene of confusion and discord. The bands of civil society are broken; the authority of government weakened, and in some instances taken away: Individuals are deprived of their liberty; their property is frequently invaded by violence, and not a single Magistrate has had courage or virtue enough to interpose. From this distressed situation it was hoped, that the wisdom and prudence of the Congress lately assembled at Philadelphia, would have delivered us. The eyes of all men were turned to them. We ardently expected that some prudent scheme of accommodating our unhappy disputes with the Mother-Country, would have been adopted and pursued. But alas! they are broken up without ever attempting it: they have taken no one step that tended to peace: they have gone on from bad to worse, and have either ignorantly misunderstood, carelessly neglected, or basely betrayed the interests of all the Colonies. . . .

. . . [M]y first business shall be to point out to you some

of the consequences that will probably follow from the Non-importation, Nonexportation, and Non-consumption Agreements, which they have adopted, and which they have ordered to be enforced in the most arbitrary manner, and under the severest penalties. On this subject, I choose to address my-self principally to You the Farmers of the Province of New-York, because I am most nearly connected with you . . . ; and also, because the interest of the farmers in general will be more sensibly affected, and more deeply injured by these agreements, than the interest of any other body of people on the continent. . . . Farmers are of the greatest benefit to the state, of any people in it: They furnish food for the merchant, and mechanic; the raw materials for most manufactures, the staple exports of the country, are the produce of their industry: be then convinced of your own importance, and think and act accordingly.

The Non-importation Agreement adopted by the Congress is to take place the first day of December next; after which no goods, wares, or merchandize, are to be imported from Great Britain or Ireland; no East-India Tea from any part of the world; no molasses, syrups, paneles, coffee, or pimento, from our islands in the West-Indies; no wine from Madeira, or the Western-Islands; no foreign indigo.

The Non-Exportation Agreement is to take effect on the tenth day of September next; after which we are not to export, directly or indirectly, any merchandize or commodity whatsoever to Great-Britain, Ireland, or the West-Indies, except RICE to Europe,—unless the several acts and parts of acts of the British Parliament, referred to by the fourth article of Association, be repealed.

The Non-consumption Agreement is to be in force the first day of March next; after which we are not to purchase or use any East-India Tea whatsoever; nor any goods, wares, or merchandize from Great-Britain or Ireland, imported after the first of December, nor molasses . . . from the West-Indies; nor wine from Madeira, or the Western Islands, nor foreign indigo.

Let us now consider the probable consequences of these agreements, supposing they should take place, and be exactly adhered to. The first I shall mention is, clamours, discord, confusion, mobs, riots, insurrections, rebellions, in Great-Britain, Ireland, and the West-Indies. . . . Congress certainly intended it should happen in some degree, or the effect they propose from these agreements cannot possibly take place. They intend to distress the manufacturers in Great-Britain, by depriving them of employment—to distress the inhabitants of Ireland . . . —to distress the West-India people. . . .

But where is the justice, where is the policy of this procedure? The manufacturers of Great-Britain, the inhabitants of Ireland, and of the West-Indies, have done us no injury. They have been no ways instrumental in bringing our distresses upon us. . . . Shall we, without any provocation, tempt or force them into riots and insurrections which must be attended with the ruin of many—probably with the death of some of them? . . . Because the ill-projected, ill-conducted, abominable scheme of some of the colonists, to form a republican government independent of Great-Britain, cannot otherwise succeed?—Good God! . . . Whatever the Gentlemen of the Congress may think of the matter, the spirit that dictated such a measure, was not the spirit of humanity.

Next let us consider the policy, or rather impolicy of this measure. Instead of conciliating, it will alienate the affections of the people of Great-Britain. Of friends it will make them our enemies; it will excite the resentment of the government at home against us; and their resentment will do us no good, but, on the contrary, much harm.

Can we think to threaten, and bully, and frighten the supreme government of the nation into a compliance with our demands? Can we expect to force a submission to our peevish and petulant humours, by exciting clamors and riots in England? We ought to know the temper and spirit, the power and strength of the nation better. A single campaign, should she exert her force, would ruin us effectually. But should she choose less violent means, she has it in her power to humble us without hurting herself. She might raise immense revenues, by laying duties in England, Ireland and the West-Indies, and we could have no remedy left; for this non-importation scheme cannot last forever. She can embarrass our trade in the Mediterranean with Spain, Holland . . . nor can we help ourselves; for whatever regulations she should make, would effectually be enforced, by the same Navy that she keeps in readiness to protect her own trade.

We shall also, probably, raise the resentment of the Irish and West-Indians. The passions of human nature are much the same in all countries. If they find us disposed wantonly to distress them, to serve our own purposes, will they not look out for some method to do without us? . . .

When a trading people carelesly neglect, or wilfully give up any branch of their trade, it is seldom in their power to recover it. Should the Irish turn their trade for flax-seed to Quebec; and the West-Indians get their flour, horses . . . from thence, or other places; the loss to the farmers of this province would be immense. . . .

You know, my Friends, that the sale of your seed not only pays your taxes, but furnishes you with many of the little conveniencies, and comforts of life; the loss of it for one year would be of more damage to you, than paying the three-penny duty on tea for twenty. . . .

. . . The loss of the sale of your seed only for one year,

would be a considerable damage to you. And yet the Congress have been so inattentive to your interest, that they have laid you under, almost, an absolute necessity of losing it the next year. . . .

. . . We have no trade but under the protection of Great-Britain. We can trade no where but where she pleases. We have no influence abroad, no ambassadors, no consuls, no fleet to protect our ships in passing the seas, nor our merchants and people in foreign countries. Should our mad schemes take place, our sailors, ship-carpenters, carmen, sail-makers, riggers, miners, smelters, forge-men, and workers in bar-iron, would be immediately out of employ; and we should have twenty mobs and riots in our own country, before one would happen in Britain or Ireland. Want of food will make these people mad, and they will come in troops upon our farms, and take that by force which they have not money to purchase. And who could blame them? Justice, indeed, might hang them; but the sympathetic eye would drop the tear of humanity on their grave.

The next thing I shall take notice of, is the advanced prices of goods, which will, not only probably, but necessarily, follow, as soon as the non-importation from Great Britain . . . shall take effect. This is a consequence that most nearly concerns you; nor can you prevent it. . . . What will you do when the prices of goods are advanced a quarter, for instance, or an half? To say that the prices of goods will not be raised, betrays your ignorance and folly. The price of any commodity always rises in proportion to the demand for it; and the demand always increases in proportion to its scarcity. As soon as the importation ceases in New-York, the quantity of goods will be daily lessened, by daily consumption; and the prices will gradually rise in proportion. "But the merchants of New-York have declared that, they will demand only a reasonable profit." Who is to judge what a reasonable profit is? Why, the merchants. Will they expose their invoices, and the secrets of their trade to you, that you may judge whether their profits are reasonable or not? Certainly they will not. . . .

I know not how it happens, but not only the merchants, but the generality of citizens, treat us countrymen with very undeserved contempt. They act as though they thought, that all wisdom, all knowledge, all understanding and sense, centered in themselves, and that we farmers were utterly ignorant of every thing, but just to drive our oxen, and to follow the plough. We are never consulted, but when they cannot do without us. And then, all the plans are laid in the City before they are offered to us. . . .

. . . We Countrymen are in this situation. No more goods can be imported: the merchants have us at their mercy: let them set their price ever so high, necessity will oblige us to come to their terms. . . .

Look well to yourselves, I beseech you. From the day that the exports from this province are stopped, the farmers may date the commencement of their ruin. Can you live without money? Will the shop-keeper give you his goods? Will the weaver, shoemaker, blacksmith, carpenter, work for you without pay? If they will, it is more than they will do for me. And unless you can sell your produce, how are you to get money? Nor will the case be better, if you are obliged to sell your produce at an under-rate. . . . [T]his is the least part of the distress that will come upon you.

Unhappily, many of you are in debt, and obliged to pay the enormous interest of seven pounds on the hundred, for considerable sums. It matters not whether your debts have been contracted through necessity, or carelesness: . . . You have had his money, and are obliged, in justice, to pay him the principal and interest, according to agreement. But without selling your produce, you can neither pay the one, nor the other; the consequence will be that after a while, a process of law will be commenced against you, and your farms must be sold by execution; and then you will have to pay not only principal and interest, but Sheriffs fees, Lawyers fees, and a long list of et caeteras.

. . . Think a little, and then tell me—when the Congress adopted this cursed scheme, did they in the least consider your interest? No, impossible! they ignorantly misunderstood, carelesly neglected, or basely betrayed you. . . .

Consider now the situation you will be in, if Great-Britain, provoked by your Non-Importation Agreement, should shut up our ports; or should the Non-Exportation agreed to by the Congress, take effect. In that case you will not be able to sell your produce: you cannot pay even the interest of the money you are indebted for: your farms must be sold, and you and your families turned out, to beggary and wretchedness.—Blessed fruits of Non-Importation and Non-Exportation! The farmer that is in debt, will be ruined: the farmer that is clear in the world, will be obliged to run in debt, to support his family: and while the proud merchant, and the forsworn smuggler, riot in their ill-gotten wealth; the laborious farmers, the grand support of every well-regulated country, must all go to the dogs together.—Vile! Shamefull! Diabolical Device!

Let us now attend a little to the Non-Consumption Agreement, which the Congress, in their Association, have imposed upon us. . . .

Will you submit to this slavish regulation?—You must.— Our sovereign Lords and Masters, the High and Mighty Delegates, in Grand Continental Congress assembled, have ordered and directed it. They have directed the Committees in the respective colonies, to establish such further regulations as they may think proper, for carrying their association, of which this Non-consumption agreement is a part, into execution. . . . The business of the Committee so chosen is to be, to inspect the conduct of the inhabitants, and see whether they violate the Association. . . . If they do, their names are to be published in the Gazette, that they may be publickly known, and universally contemned, as foes to the Rights of British America, and enemies of American Liberty.—And then the parties of the said Association will respectively break off all dealings with him or her.—In plain English,—They shall be considered as Out-laws, unworthy of the protection of civil society, and delivered over to the vengeance of a lawless, outrageous mob, to be tarred, feathered, hanged, drawn, quartered, and burnt.—O rare American Freedom! . . .

Will you be instrumental in bringing the most abject slavery on yourselves? Will you choose such Committees? Will you submit to them, should they be chosen by the weak, foolish, turbulent part of the country people?—Do as you please: but, by HIM that made me, I will not.—No, if I must be enslaved, let it be by a KING at least, and not by a parcel of upstart lawless Committee-men. If I must be devoured, let me be devoured by the jaws of a lion, and not gnawed to death by rats and vermin.

Did you choose your supervisors for the purpose of inslaving you? What right have they to fix up advertisements to call you together, for a very different purpose from that for which they were elected? Are our supervisors our masters?— And should half a dozen foolish people meet together again, in consequence of their advertisements, and choose themselves to be a Committee, as they did in many districts, in the affair of choosing Delegates, are we obliged to submit to such a Committee?—You ought, my friends, to assert your own freedom. Should such another attempt be made upon you, assemble yourselves together: tell your supervisor, that he has exceeded his commission: That you will have no such Committees:—That you are Englishmen, and will maintain your rights and privileges, and will eat, and drink, and wear, whatever the public laws of your country permit, without asking leave of any illegal, tyrannical Congress or Committee on earth. . . .

Think me not too severe. Anarchy and Confusion, Violence and Oppression, distress my country; and I must, and will speak. Though the open violator of the laws may escape punishment, through the pusillanimity of the magistrates, he shall feel the lash of my pen: and he shall feel it again and again, till remorse shall sting his guilty conscience, and shame cover his opprobrious head.

But perhaps you will say, that these men are contending for our rights; that they are defending our liberties; and though they act against law, yet that the necessity of the times will justify them. . . . These men defend our rights, and liberties, who act in open defiance of the laws? No. They are making us the most abject slaves that ever existed. The necessity of the times justify them in violating the first principles of civil society! Who induced this necessity? Who involved the province in discord, anarchy and confusion? These very men. They created that necessity, which they now plead in their own justification.

Let me intreat you, my Friends, to have nothing to do with these men, or with any of the same stamp. Peace and quietness suit you best. Confusion, and Discord, and Violence, and War, are sure destruction to the farmer. . . . Renounce all dependence on Congresses, and Committees. They have neglected, or betrayed your interests. Turn then your eyes to your constitutional representatives. They are the true, and legal, and have been hitherto, the faithful defenders of your rights, and liberties; and you have no reason to think but that they will ever be so. They will probably soon meet in General Assembly. Address yourselves to them. They are the proper persons to obtain redress of any grievances that you can justly complain of. You can trust their wisdom and prudence, that they will use the most reasonable, constitutional, and effectual methods of restoring that peace and harmony, between Great Britain and this province, which is so earnestly wished for by all good men, and which is so absolutely necessary for the happiness of us all. . . .

And whatever you may be taught by designing men, to think of the government at home, they, I am certain, would embrace us with the arms of friendship; they would press us to their bosoms, to their hearts, would we give them a fair opportunity. This opportunity our Assembly alone can give them. And this opportunity, I trust, they will give them, unless we prevent all possibility of accommodation, by our own perverseness, and ill conduct. And then, God only knows where our distresses may terminate.

NOVEMBER 16, 1774.

A. W. FARMER.

A Full Vindication of the Measures of the Congress, by Alexander Hamilton (1774)

Friends and Countrymen,

It was hardly to be expected that any man could be so presumptuous, as openly to controvert the equity, wisdom, and authority of the measures, adopted by the congress: an assembly truly respectable on every account! Whether we consider the characters of the men, who composed it; the number, and dignity of their constituents, or the important ends for which they were appointed. But, however improbable such a degree of presumption might have seemed, we find there are some, in whom it exists. Attempts are daily making to diminish the influence of their decisions, and prevent the salutary effects, intended by them. The impotence of such insidious efforts is evident from the general indignation they are treated with; so that no material ill-consequences can be dreaded from them. But lest they should have a tendency to mislead, and prejudice the minds of a few; it cannot be deemed altogether useless to bestow some notice upon them. . . .

A little consideration will convince us, that the congress instead of having "ignorantly misunderstood, carelessly neglected, or basely betrayed the interests of the colonies," have, on the contrary, devised and recommended the *only* effectual means to secure the freedom, and establish the future prosperity of America upon a solid basis. . . .

Before I proceed to confirm this assertion by the most obvious arguments, I will premise a few brief remarks. The only distinction between freedom and slavery consists in this: In the former state, a man is governed by the laws to which he has given his consent, either in person, or by his representative: In the latter, he is governed by the will of another. In the one case his life and property are his own, in the other, they depend upon the pleasure of a master. It is easy to discern which of these two states is preferable. No man in his senses can hesitate in choosing to be free, rather than a slave.

That Americans are intitled to freedom, is incontestible upon every rational principle. All men have one common original: they participate in one common nature, and consequently have one common right. No reason can be assigned why one man should exercise any power, or pre-eminence over his fellow creatures more than another; unless they have voluntarily vested him with it. Since then, Americans have not by any act of their's impowered the British Parliament to make laws for them, it follows they can have no just authority to do it.

Besides the clear voice of natural justice in this respect, the fundamental principles of the English constitution are in our favour. It has been repeatedly demonstrated, that the idea of legislation, or taxation, when the subject is not represented, is inconsistent with *that*. . . .

Every subterfuge that sophistry has been able to invent, to evade or obscure this truth, has been refuted by the most conclusive reasonings; so that we may pronounce it a matter of undeniable certainty, that the pretensions of Parliament are contradictory to the law of nature, subversive of the British constitution, and destructive of the faith of the most solemn compacts.

What then is the subject of our controversy with the mother country? It is this, whether we shall preserve that security to our lives and properties, which the law of nature, the genius of the British constitution, and our charters afford us; or whether we shall resign them into the hands of the British House of Commons, which is no more privileged to dispose of them than the Grand Mogul? What can actuate those men, who labour to delude any of us into an opinion, that the object of contention between the parent state and the colonies is only three pence duty upon tea? or that the commotions in America originate in a plan, formed by some turbulent men to erect it into a republican government? The parliament claims a right to tax us in all cases whatsoever: Its late acts are in virtue of that claim. How ridiculous then is it to affirm, that we are quarrelling for the trifling sum of three pence a pound on tea; when it is evidently the principle against which we contend.

The design of electing members to represent us in general congress, was, that the wisdom of America might be collected in devising the most proper and expedient means to repel this atrocious invasion of our rights. It has been accordingly done. Their decrees are binding upon all, and demand a religious observance. . . .

. . . [I]t is become in some measure necessary to vindicate the conduct of this venerable assembly from the aspersions of men, who are their adversaries, only because they are foes to America.

When the political salvation of any community is depending, it is incumbent upon those who are set up as its guardians, to embrace such measures, as have justice, vigour, and a probability of success to recommend them: If instead of this, they take those methods which are in themselves feeble, and little likely to succeed; and may, through a defect in vigour, involve the community in still greater danger; they may be justly considered as its betrayers. It is not enough in times of eminent peril to use only possible means of preservation: Justice and sound policy dictate the use of probable means.

The only scheme of opposition, suggested by those, who have been, and are averse from a non-importation and non-exportation agreement, is, by Remonstrance and Petition. The authors and abettors of this scheme, have never been able to *invent* a single argument to prove the likelihood of its succeeding. On the other hand, there are many standing facts, and valid considerations against it.

In the infancy of the present dispute, we had recourse to this method only. We addressed the throne in the most loyal and respectful manner, in a legislative capacity; but what was the consequence? Our address was treated with contempt and neglect. The first American congress did the same, and met with similar treatment. The total repeal of the stamp act, and the partial repeal of the revenue acts took place, not because the complaints of America were deemed just and reasonable; but because these acts were found to militate against the commercial interests of Great Britain: This was the declared motive of the repeal.

These instances are sufficient for our purpose; but they derive greater validity and force from the following:

The legal assembly of Massachusetts Bay, presented, not long since, a most humble, dutiful, and earnest petition to his Majesty, requesting the dismission of a governor, highly odious to the people, and whose misrepresentations they regarded as one chief source of all their calamities. Did they succeed in their request? No, it was treated with the greatest indignity, and stigmatized as "a seditious, vexatious, and scandalous libel."

I know the men I have to deal with will acquiesce in this stigma. Will they also dare to calumniate the noble and spirited petition that came from the Mayor and Aldermen of the city of London? Will they venture to justify that unparalelled stride of power, by which popery and arbitrary dominion were established in Canada? The citizens of London remonstrated against it; they signified its repugnancy to the principles of the revolution; but like ours, their complaints were unattended to. From thence we may learn how little dependence ought to be placed on this method of obtaining the redress of grievances.

There is less reason now than ever to expect deliverance, in this way, from the hand of oppression. The system of slavery, fabricated against America, cannot at this time be considered as the effect of inconsideration and rashness. It is the offspring of mature deliberation. . . .

What can we represent which has not already been represented? what petitions can we offer, that have not already been offered? The rights of America, and the injustice of parliamentary pretensions have been clearly and repeatedly stated, both in and out of parliament. No new arguments can be framed to operate in our favour. . . .

This being the case, we can have no resource but in a restriction of our trade, or in a resistance *vi & armis*. It is impossible to conceive any other alternative. Our congress, therefore, have imposed what restraint they thought necessary. Those, who condemn or clamour against it, do nothing more, nor less, than advise us to be slaves.

I shall now examine the principal measures of the congress, and vindicate them fully from the charge of injustice or impolicy. . . .

. . . Though the manufacturers of Great Britain and Ireland, and the Inhabitants of the West Indies are not chargeable with any actual crime towards America, they may, in a political view, be esteemed criminal. In a civil society, it is the duty of each particular branch to promote, not only the good of the whole community, but the good of every other particular branch: If one part endeavours to violate the rights of another, the rest ought to assist in preventing the injury: When they do not, but remain neutral, they are deficient in their duty, and may be regarded, in some measure, as accomplices. . . .

Since then the persons who will be distressed by the methods we are using for our own protection, have by their neutrality first committed a breach of an obligation, similar to that which bound us to consult their emolument, it is plain, the obligation upon us is annulled, and we are blameless in what we are about to do.

With respect to the manufacturers of Great Britain, they are criminal in a more particular sense. Our oppression arises from that member of the great body politic, of which they compose a considerable part. So far as their influence has been wanting to counteract the iniquity of their rulers, so far they acquiesced in it, and are to be deemed confederates in their guilt. It is impossible to exculpate a people, that suffers its rulers to abuse and tyrannize over others.

It may not be amiss to add, that we are ready to receive with open arms, any who may be sufferers by the operation of our measures, and recompense them with every blessing our country affords to honest industry. We will receive them as brethren, and make them sharers with us in all the advantages we are struggling for.

From these plain and indisputable principles, the mode of opposition we have chosen is reconcileable to the strictest maxims of Justice. It remains now to be examined, whether it has also the sanction of good policy.

To render it agreeable to good policy, three things are requisite. First, that the necessity of the times require it: Secondly, that it be not the probable source of greater evils, than those it pretends to remedy: And lastly, that it have a probability of success.

That the necessity of the times demands it needs but little elucidation. We are threatened with absolute slavery; it has been proved, . . . and of course, that a restriction on our trade, is the only peaceable method, in our power, to avoid the impending mischief: It follows therefore, that such a restriction is necessary.

That it is not the probable source of greater evils than those it pretends to remedy, may easily be determined. The most abject slavery, which comprehends almost every species of human misery, is what it is designed to prevent.

The consequences of the means are a temporary stagnation of commerce, and thereby a deprivation of the luxuries and some of the conveniencies of life. The necessaries, and many of the conveniencies, our own fertile and propitious soil affords us.

No person, that has enjoyed the sweets of liberty, can be insensible of its infinite value, or can reflect on its reverse, without horror and detestation. No person, that is not lost to every generous feeling of humanity, or that is not stupidly blind to his own interest, could bear to offer himself and posterity as victims at the shrine of despotism, in preference to enduring the short lived inconveniencies that may result from an abridgment, or even entire suspension of commerce.

Were not the disadvantages of slavery too obvious to stand in need of it, I might enumerate and describe the tedious train of calamities, inseparable from it. I might shew that it is fatal to religion and morality; that it tends to debase the mind, and corrupt its noblest springs of action. I might shew, that it relaxes the sinews of industry, clips the wings of commerce, and introduces misery and indigence in every shape.

Under the auspices of tyranny, the life of the subject is often sported with; and the fruits of his daily toil are consumed in oppressive taxes, that serve to gratify the ambition, avarice and lusts of his superiors. Every court minion riots in the spoils of the honest labourer, and despises the hand by which he is fed. The page of history is replete with instances that loudly warn us to beware of slavery. . . .

The evils which may flow from the execution of our measures, if we consider them with respect to their extent and duration, are comparatively nothing. In all human probability they will scarcely be felt. Reason and experience teach us, that the consequences would be too fatal to Great Britain to admit of delay. There is an immense trade between her and the colonies. The revenues arising from thence are prodigious. The consumption of her manufactures in these colonies supplies the means of subsistence to a vast number of her most useful inhabitants. The experiment we have made heretofore, shews us of how much importance our commercial connexion is to her; and gives us the highest assurance of obtaining immediate redress by suspending it.

From these considerations it is evident, she must do something decisive. She must either listen to our complaints, and restore us to a peaceful enjoyment of our violated rights; or she must exert herself to enforce her despotic claims by fire and sword. To imagine she would prefer the latter, implies a charge of the grossest infatuation of madness itself. Our numbers are very considerable; the courage of Americans has been tried and proved. Contests for liberty have ever been found the most bloody, implacable and obstinate. The disciplined troops Great Britain could send against us, would be but few, Our superiority in number would over balance our inferiority in discipline. It would be a hard, if not an impracticable task to subjugate us by force.

Besides, while Great Britain was engaged in carrying on an unnatural war against us, her commerce would be in a state of decay. Her revenues would be decreasing. An armament, sufficient to enslave America, would put her to an insupportable expence.

She would be laid open to the attacks of foreign enemies. Ruin, like a deluge, would pour in from every quarter. After lavishing her blood and treasure to reduce us to a state of vassalage, she would herself become a prey to some triumphant neighbour.

These are not imaginary mischiefs. The colonies contain above three millions of people. Commerce flourshes with the most rapid progress throughout them. This commerce Great-Britain has hitherto regulated to her own advantage. Can we think the annihilation of so exuberant a source of wealth, a matter of trifling import. On the contrary, must it not be productive of the most disastrous effects? It is evident it must. It is equally evident, that the conquest of so numerous a people, armed in the animating cause of liberty could not be accomplished without an inconceivable expence of blood and treasure.

We cannot therefore suspect Great-Britain to be capable of such frantic extravagance as to hazard these dreadful consequences; without which she must necessarily desist from her unjust pretensions, and leave us in the undisturbed possession of our privileges. . . .

But should we admit a possibility of a third course, as our pamphleteer supposes, that is, the endeavouring to bring us to a compliance by putting a stop to our whole trade: Even this would not be so terrible as he pretends. We can live without trade of any kind. Food and clothing we have within ourselves. Our climate produces cotton, wool, flax and hemp, which, with proper cultivation would furnish us with summer apparel in abundance. The article of cotton indeed would do more, it would contribute to defend us from the inclemency of winter. We have sheep, which, with due care in improving and increasing them, would soon yield a sufficiency of wool. The large quantity of skins, we have among us, would never let us want a warm and comfortable suit. It would be no unbecoming employment for our daughters to provide silks of their own country. The silk-worm answers as well here as in any part of the world. Those hands, which may be deprived of business by the cessation of commerce, may be occupied in various kinds of manufactures and other internal improvements. If by the necessity of the thing, manufactures should once be established and take root among us, they will pave the way, still more, to the future grandeur and glory of America, and by lessening its need of external commerce, will render it still securer against the encroachments of tyranny. . . .

I come now to consider the last and principal engredient that constitutes the policy of a measure, which is a probability of success. . . .

The design of the Congress in their proceedings, it cannot, and need not be desired, was either, by a prospect of the evil consequences, to influence the ministry to give up their enterprize; or should they prove inflexible, to affect the inhabitants of Great-Britain, Ireland and the West-Indies in such a manner, as to rouse them from their state of neutrality, and engage them to unite with us in opposing the lawless hand of tyranny, which is extended to ravish our liberty from us, and might soon be extended for the same purpose against them.

The Farmer mentions, as one probable consequence of our measures, "clamours, discord, confusion, mobs, riots, insurrections, rebellions in Great-Britain, Ireland and the West-Indies;" though at the same time that he thinks it is, he also thinks it is not a probable consequence. For my part, without hazarding any such seeming contradictions, I shall, in a plain way, assert, that I verily believe a non-importation and non-exportation will effect all the purposes they are intended for.

It is no easy matter to make any tolerably exact estimate of the advantages that acrue to Great-Britain, Ireland and the West-Indies from their commercial intercourse with the colonies, nor indeed is it necessary. Every man, the least acquainted with the state and extent of our trade, must be convinced, it is the source of immense revenues to the parent state, and gives employment and bread to a vast number of his Majesty's subjects. It is impossible but that a suspension of it for any time, must introduce beggary and wretchedness in an eminent degree, both in England and Ireland; and as to the West-India plantations, they could not possibly subsist without us. I am the more confident of this, because I have a pretty general acquaintance with their circumstances and dependencies. . . .

The omnipotence and all sufficiency of Great-Britain may be pretty good topics for her passionate admirers to exercise their declamatory powers upon, for amusement and trial of skill; but they ought not to be proposed to the world as matters of truth and reality. In the calm, unprejudiced eye of reason, they are altogether visionary. As to her wealth, it is notorious that she is oppressed with a heavy national debt, which it requires the utmost policy and economy ever to discharge. Luxury has arrived to a great pitch; and it is an universal maxim that luxury indicates the declension of a state. Her subjects are loaded with the most enormous taxes: All circumstances agree in declaring their distress. The continual emigrations, from Great-Britain and Ireland, to the continent, are a glaring symptom, that those kingdoms are a good deal impoverished.

The attention of Great-Britain has hitherto been constantly awake to expand her commerce. She has been vigilant to explore every region, with which it might be her interest to trade. One of the principal branches of her commerce is with the colonies. These colonies, as they are now settled and peopled, have been the work of near two centuries: They are blessed with every advantage of soil, climate and situation. They have advanced with an almost incredible rapidity. It is therefore an egregious piece of absurdity to affirm, that the loss of our trade would be felt for a time (which must signify a short time.) No new schemes could be pursued that would not require, at least, as much time to repair the loss of our trade, as was spent in bringing it to its present degree of perfection, which is near two centuries. Nor can it be reasonably imagined, that the total and sudden loss of so extensive and lucrative a branch, would not produce the most violent effects to a nation that subsists entirely upon its commerce. . . .

. . . It is said, that "instead of conciliating, we shall alienate the affections of the people of Great-Britain, of friends, we shall make them our enemies;" and further, that "we shall excite the resentment of the government at home against us, which will do us no good, but, on the contrary, much harm."

Soon after, we are told that "we shall probably raise the resentment of the Irish and West-Indians. . . ."

To these objections I reply, first with respect to the inhabitants of Great-Britain, that if they are our friends, as is supposed, and as we have reason to believe; they cannot, without being destitute of rationality, be incensed against us for using the only peaceable and probable means, in our power, to pre-serve our invaded rights: They know by their own experience how fruitless remonstrances and petitions are: They know, we have tried them over and over to no purpose: They know also, how dangerous to their liberties, the loss of ours must be. What then could exite their resentment if they have the least regard to common justice? The calamities, that threaten them, proceed from the weakness, or wickedness of their own rul-ers; which compels us to take the measures we do. The insin-uation, that we wantonly distress them to serve our own purposes, is futile and unsupported by a single argument. . . .

The same may be said with regard to the Irish and the West-Indians, which has been said concerning the people of Great-Britain. The Irish, in particular, by their own circum-stances will be taught to sympathise with us, and commend our conduct. Justice will direct their resentment to its proper objects. . . .

There is one argument I have frequently heard urged, which it may be of some use to invalidate. It is this, that if the mother country should be inclined to an accommodation of our disputes, we have by our rash procedure thrown an insur-mountable obstacle in her way; we have made it disgraceful to her to comply with our requisitions, because they are pro-posed in a hostile manner.

Our present measures, I have proved, are the only peace-able ones we could place the least confidence in. They are the least exceptionable, upon the score of irritating Great-Britain, of any our circumstances would permit. . . .

I have omitted many considerations, which might be ad-duced to shew the impolicy of Great-Britains, delaying to ac-commodate matters, and attempting to enforce submission by cutting off all external sources of trade. To say all the subject allows, would spin out this piece to an immoderate length; I shall, therefore, content myself with mentioning only three things more. First, it would be extremely hurtful to the commerce of Great-Britain to drive us to the necessity of laying a regular foundation for manufactories of our own; which, if once established, could not easily, if at all, be undermined, or abolished. Secondly, it would be very expensive to the nation to maintain a fleet for the purpose of blocking up our ports, and destroying our trade: nor could she interrupt our intercourse with foreign climes without, at the same time, retrenching her own revenues; for she must then lose the duties and customs upon the articles we are wont to export to, and import from them. Added to this, it would not be prudent to risk the displeasure of those nations, to whom our trade is useful and beneficial. And lastly, a perseverance in ill-treatment would naturally beget such deep-rooted animosities in America, as might never be eradicated; and which might operate to the prejudice of the empire to the latest period.

Thus have I clearly proved, that the plan of opposition concerted by our congress is perfectly consonant with justice and sound policy; and will, in all human probability, secure our freedom against the assaults of our enemies.

But, after all, it may be demanded why they have adopted a non-exportation; seeing many arguments tend to shew that a non-importation alone would accomplish the end desired?

I answer, that the continuance of our exports is the only thing which could lessen, or retard the efficacy of a non-importation. It is not indeed probable it should do that to any great degree; but it was adviseable to provide against every possible obstruction. Besides this, the prospect of its taking place, and of the evils attendant upon it, will be a prevailing motive with the ministry to abandon their malignant schemes.

It will also serve to convince them, that we are not afraid of putting ourselves to any inconveniencies, sooner than be the victims of their lawless ambition.

The execution of this measure has been wisely deferred to a future time, because we have the greatest reason to think affairs will be settled without it, and because its consequences would be too fatal to be justified by any thing but absolute necessity. This necessity there will be, should not our disputes terminate before the time allotted for its commencement.

Before I conclude this part of my address, I will answer two very singular interrogatories proposed by the Farmer, "Can we think (says he) to threaten, and bully, and frighten the supreme government of the nation into a compliance with our demands? Can we expect to force submission to our peevish and petulant humours, by exciting clamours and riots in England?" No, gentle Sir. We neither desire, nor endeavour to threaten, bully, or frighten any persons into a compliance with our demands. We have no peevish and petulant humours to be submitted to. All we aim at, is to convince your high and mighty masters, the ministry, that we are not such asses as to let them ride us as they please. We are determined to shew them, that we know the value of freedom; nor shall their rapacity extort, that inestimable jewel from us, without a manly and virtuous struggle. But for your part, sweet Sir! tho' we cannot much applaud your wisdom, yet we are compelled to admire your valour, which leads you to hope you may be able to swear, threaten, bully and frighten all America into a compliance with your sinister designs. When properly accoutered and armed with your formidable hiccory cudgel, what may not the ministry expect from such a champion? alas! for the poor committee gentlemen, how I tremble when I reflect on the many wounds and scars they must receive from your tremendous arm! Alas! for their supporters and abettors; a very large part indeed of the continent; but what of that? they must all be soundly drubbed with that con-founded hiccory cudgel; for surely you would not undertake to drub one of them, without knowing yourself able to treat all their friends and adherents in the same manner; since 'tis plain you would bring them all upon your back. . . .

A FRIEND TO AMERICA.

The Farmer Refuted,
by Alexander Hamilton (1775)

I resume my pen, in reply to the curious epistle, you have
been pleased to favour me with; and can assure you, that, notwithstanding, I am naturally of a grave and phlegmatic disposition, it has been the source of abundant merriment to me.
The spirit that breathes throughout is so rancorous, illiberal
and imperious: The argumentative part of it so puerile and
fallacious: The misrepresentations of facts so palpable and
flagrant: The criticisms so illiterate, trifling and absurd: The
conceits so low, steril and splenetic, that I will venture to pronounce it one of the most ludicrous performances, which has
been exhibited to public view, during all the present controversy.

You have not even imposed the laborious task of pursuing
you through a labyrinth of *subtilty*. You have not had ability
sufficient, however violent your efforts, to try the *depths* of
sophistry; but have barely skimmed along its *surface*. I should,
almost, deem the animadversions, I am going to make, unnecessary, were it not, that, without them, you might exult in
a fancied victory, and arrogate to yourself imaginary trophies.

But while I pass this judgment, it is not my intention to
detract from your real merit. Candour obliges me to acknowledge, that you possess every accomplishment of a polemical

writer, which may serve to dazzle and mislead superficial and vulgar minds; a peremptory dictatorial air, a pert vivacity of expression, an inordinate passion for conceit, and a noble disdain of being fettered by the laws of truth. These, Sir, are important qualifications, and these all unite in you, in a very eminent degree. So that, though you may never expect the plaudit of the judicious and discerning, you may console yourself, with this assurance, that

> Fools and witlings "will" ev'ry sentence raise,
> And wonder, with a foolish face of praise.

. . .

Having thus, briefly, delivered my sentiments of your performance in general, I shall proceed to a particular examination of it, so far, as may be requisite, towards placing it in that just point of light in which it ought to stand. I flatter myself, I shall find no difficulty in obviating the objections you have produced, against the Full Vindication; and in shewing, that your View of the Controversy between Great-Britain and the Colonies, is not only partial and unjust, but diametrically opposite to the first principles of civil society. In doing this, I may, occasionally, interweave some strictures on the Congress Canvassed.

First, then, I observe, you endeavour to bring the imputation of inconsistency upon me, for writing "a long and elaborate pamphlet to justify decisions against whose influence none but *impotent* attempts had been made." A little attention would have unfolded the whole mystery. The reason assigned, for what I did, was, "lest those attempts," impotent as they were in a general sense, "might, yet, have a tendency to mislead and prejudice the minds of a few." To prevent this, I wrote; and if I have been instrumental in preserving a single person, from the baneful effects of your insidious efforts, I shall not regret the time I have devoted to that laudable purpose. To confirm, or to add one friend to his country, would afford a more refined and permanent satisfaction to me, than could, possibly, animate the breast of the proudest ministerial minion, though elevated to the pinnacle of his wished-for preferment, and basking in the sunshine of court favour, as the despicable wages of his prostitution and servility.

You tell me, "I knew that at the bar of impartial reason and common sense, the conduct of the Congress must be condemned; but was too much interested, too deeply engaged, in party-views and party-heats, to bear this with patience. I had no remedy (you say) but *artifice, sophistry, misrepresentation,* and *abuse.* These (you call) my weapons, and these I wield, like an old experienced practitioner."

You ask, "Is this too heavy a charge? Can you lay your hand upon your heart, and, upon your honour, plead not guilty?" Yes, Sir, I can do more. I can make a solemn appeal to the tribunal of Heaven, for the rectitude of my intentions. I can affirm, with the most scrupulous regard to truth, that I am of opinion, the conduct of the Congress will bear the most impartial scrutiny, that I am not interested, more, than as the felicity and prosperity of this vast continent are concerned, and that I am perfectly disengaged from party of every kind.

Here, I expect, you will exclaim with your usual vehemence and indecency; you are now espousing the cause of a party! It is the most daring impudence and falshood to assert the contrary! I can, by no means, conceive, that an opposition to a small herd of mal-contents, among whom, you have thought proper to rank, and a zealous attachment to the general measures of America can be denominated the effect of a party spirit. You, Sir, and your adherents may be justly deemed a faction, because you compose a small number inimical to the common voice of your country. To determine the truth of this affirmation, it is necessary to take a comprehensive view of all the colonies.

Th[r]oughout your letter, you seem to consider me, as a person, who has acted, and is still acting some part in the formation and execution of public measures. You tacitly represent me as a Delegate, or member of the Committee. Whether this be done with a design to create a suspicion of my sincerity, or whether it be really your opinion, I know not. Perhaps it is from a complex motive. But I can assure you, if you are in earnest, that you are entirely mistaken. I have taken no other part in the affair, than that of defending the proceedings of the Congress, in conversation, and by the pamphlet I lately published. I approved of them, and thought an undeviating compliance with them essential to the preservation of American freedom. I shall, therefore, strenuously exert myself for the promotion of that valuable end.

In the field of literary contention, it is common to see the epithets *artifice, sophistry, misrepresentation* and *abuse*, mutually bandied about. Whether they are more justly applicable to you, or me, the public must decide. With respect to abuse, I make not the least doubt, but every reader will allow you to surpass me in that. . . .

I shall, for the present, pass over to that part of your pamphlet, in which you endeavour to establish the supremacy of the British Parliament over America. After a proper eclaircissement of this point, I shall draw such inferences, as will sap the foundation of every thing you have offered.

The first thing that presents itself is a wish, that "I had, explicitly, declared to the public my ideas of the *natural rights* of mankind. Man, in a state of nature (you say) may be considered, as perfectly free from all restraints of *law* and *government*, and, then, the weak must submit to the strong."

I shall, henceforth, begin to make some allowance for that enmity, you have discovered to the *natural rights* of mankind. For, though ignorance of them in this enlightened age cannot be admitted, as a sufficient excuse for you; yet, it ought, in some measure, to extenuate your guilt. If you will follow my advice, there still may be hopes of your reformation. Apply yourself, without delay, to the study of the law of nature. I would recommend to your perusal, Grotius. Puffendorf, Locke, Montesquieu, and Burlemaqui. I might mention other excellent writers on this subject; but if you attend, diligently, to these, you will not require any others.

There is so strong a similitude between your political principles and those maintained by Mr. Hobbs, that, in judging from them, a person might very easily *mistake* you for a disciple of his. His opinion was, exactly, coincident with yours, relative to man in a state of nature. He held, as you do, that he was, then, perfectly free from all restraint of *law* and *government*. Moral obligation, according to him, is derived from the introduction of civil society; and there is no virtue, but what is purely artificial, the mere contrivance of politicians, for the maintenance of social intercourse. But the reason he run into this absurd and impious doctrine, was, that he disbelieved the existence of an intelligent superintending principle, who is the governor, and will be the final judge of the universe.

As you, sometimes, swear *by him that made you*, I conclude, your sentiment does not correspond with his, in that which is the basis of the doctrine, you both agree in; and this makes it impossible to imagine whence this congruity between you arises. To grant, that there is a supreme intelligence, who rules the world, and has established laws to regulate the actions of his creatures; and, still, to assert, that man, in a state of nature, may be considered as perfectly free from all restraints of *law* and *government*, appear to a common understanding, altogether irreconcileable.

Good and wise men, in all ages, have embraced a very dissimilar theory. They have supposed, that the deity, from the relations, we stand in, to himself and to each other, has constituted an eternal and immutable law, which is, indispensibly, obligatory upon all mankind, prior to any human institution whatever.

This is what is called the law of nature, "which, being coeval with mankind, and dictated by God himself, is, of course, superior in obligation to any other. It is binding over all the globe, in all countries, and at all times. No human laws are of any validity, if contrary to this; and such of them as are valid, derive all their authority, mediately, or immediately, from this original."

Upon this law, depend the natural rights of mankind, the supreme being gave existence to man, together with the means of preserving and beatifying that existence. He endowed him with rational faculties, by the help of which, to discern and pursue such things, as were consistent with his duty and interest, and invested him with an inviolable right to personal liberty, and personal safety.

Hence, in a state of nature, no man had any *moral* power to deprive another of his life, limbs, property or liberty; nor the least authority to command, or exact obedience from him; except that which arose from the ties of consanguinity.

Hence also, the origin of all civil government, justly established, must be a voluntary compact, between the rulers and the ruled; and must be liable to such limitations, as are necessary for the security of the *absolute rights* of the latter; for what original title can any man or set of men have, to govern others, except their own consent? To usurp dominion over a people, in their own despite, or to grasp at a more extensive power than they are willing to entrust, is to violate that law of nature, which gives every man a right to his personal liberty; and can, therefore, confer no obligation to obedience.

"The principal aim of society is to protect individuals, in the enjoyment of those absolute rights, which were vested in them by the immutable laws of nature; but which could not be preserved, in peace, without that mutual assistance, and intercourse, which is gained by the institution of friendly and social communities. Hence it follows, that the first and primary end of human laws, is to maintain and regulate these *absolute rights* of individuals."

If we examine the pretensions of parliament, by this criterion, which is evidently, a good one, we shall, presently detect their injustice. First, they are subversive of our natural liberty, because an authority is assumed over us, which we by no means assent to. And secondly, they divest us of that moral security, for our lives and properties, which we are intitled to, and which it is the primary end of society to bestow. For such security can never exist, while we have no part in making the laws, that are to bind us; and while it may be the interest of our uncontroled legislators to oppress us as much as possible.

To deny these principles will be not less absurd, than to deny the plainest axioms: I shall not, therefore, attempt any further illustration of them. . . .

The idea of colony does not involve the idea of slavery. There is a wide difference, between the dependence of a free people, and the submission of slaves. The former I allow, the latter I reject with disdain. Nor does the notion of a colony imply any subordination to our fellow subjects, in the parent state, while there is one common sovereign established. The dependence of the colonies, on Great-Britain, is an ambiguous and equivocal phrase. It may, either mean dependence on the people of Great-Britain, or on the King. In the former sense, it is absurd and unaccountable: In the latter it is just and rational. No person will affirm, that a French colony is independent, on the parent state, though it acknowledge the King of France as rightful sovereign. Nor can it, with any greater propriety, be said, that an English colony is independent, while it bears allegiance to the King of Great-Britain. The difference, between their dependence, is only that which distinguishes civil liberty from slavery; and results from the different genius of the French and English constitution.

But you deny, that "we can be liege subjects to the King of Great-Britain, while we disavow the authority of parliament." You endeavour to prove it thus, "The King of Great Britain was placed on the throne, by virtue of an act of parliament; and he is King of America, by virtue of being King of Great-Britain. He is therefore King of America by act of parliament: And, if we disclaim that authority of Parliament, which made him our King, we, in fact, reject him from being our King; for we disclaim that authority, by which he is King at all."

Admitting, that the King of Great Britain was enthroned by virtue of an act of parliament, and that he is King of America, because he is King of Great-Britain, yet the act of parliament is not the *efficient cause* of his being the King of America: It is only the *occasion* of it. He is King of America, by virtue of a compact between us and the Kings of Great-Britain. These colonies were planted and settled by the Grants, and under the Protection of English Kings, who entered into covenants with us for themselves, their heirs and successors; and it is from these covenants, that the duty of protection on their part, and the duty of allegiance on ours arise.

So that, to disclaim, the authority of a British Parliament over us, does by no means imply the dereliction of our allegiance to British Monarchs. Our compact takes no cognizance of the manner of their accession to the throne. It is sufficient for us, that they are Kings of England.

The most valid reasons can be assigned for our allegiance to the King of Great-Britain; but not one of the least force or plausibility for our subjection to parliamentary decrees.

We hold our lands in America by virtue of charters from British Monarchs; and are under no obligations to the lords or commons for them: Our title is similar and equal to that, by which they possess their lands; and the King is the legal fountain of both: this is one grand source of our obligation to allegiance.

Another, and the principal source is, that protection which we have hitherto enjoyed from the Kings of Great-Britain. Nothing is more common than to hear the votaries of parliament urge the protection we have received from the mother country, as an argument for submission to its claims. But they entertain erroneous conceptions of the matter; the King himself, being the supreme executive magistrate, is regarded by the constitution, as the supreme protector of the empire. For this purpose, he is the generalissimo, or first in military command; in him is vested the power of making war and peace, of raising armies, equipping fleets and directing all their motions. He it is that has defended us from our enemies, and to him alone, we are obliged to render allegiance and submission.

The law of nature and the British constitution both confine allegiance to the person of the King; and found it upon the principle of protection. We may see the subject discussed at large in the case of Calvin: The definition given of it by the learned Coke, is this, "Legiance is the mutual bond and obligation between the King and his subjects, whereby subjects are called his liege subjects, because they are bound to obey and serve him; and he is called their liege lord, because he is bound to maintain and defend them." Hence it is evident, that while we enjoy the protection of the King, it is incumbent upon us to obey and serve him, without the interposition of parliamentary supremacy.

The right of parliament to legislate for us cannot be accounted for upon any reasonable grounds. The constitution of Great Britain is very properly called a limitted monarchy, the people having reserved to themselves a share in the legislature, as a check upon the regal authority, to prevent its degenerating into despotism and tyranny. The very aim and intention of the democratical part, or the house of commons, is to secure the rights of the people. Its very being depends upon those rights. Its whole power is derived from them, and must be terminated by them. . . .

When I say, that the authority of parliament is confined to Great-Britain, I speak of it, in its primitive and original state. Parliament may acquire an incidental influence over others; but this must be by their own free consent. For without this, any power it might exercise, would be mere usurpation, and by no means a just authority.

The best way of determining disputes, and of investigating truth, is by descending to elementary principles. Any other method may only bewilder and misguide the understanding; but this will soon lead to a convincing and satisfactory crisis. By observing this method, we shall learn the following truths.

That the existence of the house of commons depends upon the people's right to a share in the legislature; which is exercised, by means of electing the members of that house. That the end and intention of this right is, to preserve the life, property and liberty of the subject, from the encroachments of oppression and tyranny.

That this end is accomplished, by means of the *intimate connexion* of interest, between those members and their constituents, the people of Great-Britain.

That with respect to the people of America, there is no such *intimate connexion* of interest; but the contrary. And therefore that end could not be answered to them; consequently the *end* ceasing, the *means* must cease also.

That the house of commons derives all its power, from its own real constituents, who are the people of Great-Britain, and that therefore, it has no power, but what they *originally* had in themselves.

That they had no original right to the life, property, or liberty of Americans; nor any acquired from their own consent, and of course could give no authority over them.

That, therefore, the house of commons has no such authority. . . .

Boston was the first victim to the meditated vengeance: An act was passed to block up her ports, and destroy her commerce, with every aggravating circumstance that can be imagined. It was not left at her option to elude the stroke, by paying for the tea; but she was also to make such satisfaction to the officers of his Majesty's revenue and others, who might have suffered as should be judged *reasonable by the governor*. Nor is this all, before her commerce could be restored, she must have submitted to the authority claimed and exercised by the parliament.

Had the rest of America passively looked on, while a sister colony was subjugated, the same fate would gradually have overtaken all. The safety of the whole depends upon the mutual protection of every part. If the sword of oppression be permitted to lop off one limb without opposition, reiterated strokes will soon dismember the whole body. Hence it was the duty and interest of all the colonies to succour and support the one which was suffering. It is sometimes sagaciously urged, that we ought to commisserate the distresses of the people of Massachusetts; but not intermeddle in their affairs, so far, as perhaps to bring ourselves into like circumstances with them. This might be good reasoning, if our neutrality would not be more dangerous, than our participation: But I am unable to conceive how the colonies in general would have any security against oppression, if they were once to content themselves, with barely *pitying* each other, while parliament was prosecuting and enforcing its demands. Unless they continually protect and assist each other, they must all inevitably fall a prey to their enemies. . . .

I shall conclude this head, with one more observation, which is this, That all such, as may be deprived of business, by the operation of our measures in America, may be employed in cultivating lands. We have enough, and to spare. It is of no force to object, that "when our exports are stopped, our grain would become of little worth." They can be occupied in raising other things, that will be more wanted, to wit; Materials for manufactures; and only a sufficiency of provisions, for their own use. In such a country as this, there can be no great difficulty in finding business, for all its inhabitants. Those obstacles, which to the eye of timidity or disaffection, seem like the *Alps* would to the hand of resolution and perseverance, become mere *hillocks*.

Once more I insist upon it, that Great-Britain can never force us to submission, by blocking up our ports; and that the consequences of such a procedure to herself, Ireland and the West-Indies, would be too fatal to admit of it. If she is determined to enslave us, it must be by force of arms; and to attempt this, I again assert, would be nothing less, than *the grossest infatuation, madness itself.*

Whatever may be said of the disciplined troops of Britain, the event of the contest must be extremely doubtful. There is a certain enthusiasm in liberty, that makes human nature rise above itself, in acts of bravery and heroism. It cannot be expected, that America would yield, without a magnanimous persevering and bloody struggle. The testimony of past ages, and the least knowledge of mankind, must suffice to convince us of the contrary. We have a recent instance in *Corsica*, to what lengths a people will go, in defence of its liberties; and if we take a view of the colonies in general, we must perceive that the pulse of Americans beats high, in their country's cause. Let us then suppose, the arms of Britain triumphant and America mutilated, exhausted and vanquished. What situation will Britain then be in? What laurels will she reap, from her conquest? Alas! none. Every true friend to that deluded country, must shudder at the prospect . . .

Part II

IS THE CONSTITUTION TYRANNICAL?

━━━━━━ ☆ ━━━━━━

The Debate Over Ratification

After extensive debate, the delegates to the Constitutional Convention of 1787, Hamilton among them, proposed a new constitution to address the failure of the Articles of Confederation and fulfill the promise of the American Revolution. For the document to become our governing charter, however, it first had to be ratified by the American people.

An intense public debate ensued, with two broad camps taking shape: the Federalists, including Hamilton, supported the Constitution, while the anti-Federalists, writing under the pen name Brutus, opposed it. In a series of essays called *The Federalist*, Hamilton is in his prime, arguing that the Constitution provides for the right balance of federal power and constraint. Both a strong federal government and a strong presidency will protect against anarchy, he argues, without falling prey to tyranny. Anti-Federalists pushed back, raising concerns about excessive presidential power and inadequate state power, believing the new Constitution would lead to tyranny.

Thanks in no small part to Hamilton's writings, the Federalists won. But while his arguments carried the day over the anti-Federalists', their debates remain relevant as we think about the risks to liberty posed by our system of government. Concerns about excessive state power and presidential power are still at the forefront of today's politics, just as they were when Americans debated whether to ratify the proposed Constitution in 1787. For some, Hamilton's defense of the constitutional system will help explain the genius of the American government, while others may find his words overly optimistic in retrospect about the strength of the system he helped design.

HAMILTON V. BRUTUS

(Constitution Ratification)

Brutus No. 1
(1787)

The first question that presents itself on the subject is, whether a confederated government be the best for the United States or not? Or in other words, whether the thirteen United States should be reduced to one great republic, governed by one legislature, and under the direction of one executive and judicial; or whether they should continue thirteen confederated republics, under the direction and control of a supreme federal head for certain defined national purposes only?

This enquiry is important, because, although the government reported by the convention does not go to a perfect and entire consolidation, yet it approaches so near to it, that it must, if executed, certainly and infallibly terminate in it.

This government is to possess absolute and uncontrollable power, legislative, executive and judicial, with respect to every object to which it extends, for by the last clause of section 8th, article 1st, it is declared "that the Congress shall have power to make all laws which shall be necessary and proper for carrying into execution the foregoing powers, and all other powers vested by this constitution, in the government of the United States; or in any department or office thereof." And by the 6th article, it is declared "that this constitution, and

the laws of the United States, which shall be made in pursuance thereof, and the treaties made, or which shall be made,
under the authority of the United States, shall be the supreme
law of the land; and the judges in every state shall be bound
thereby, any thing in the constitution, or law of any state to
the contrary notwithstanding." It appears from these articles
that there is no need of any intervention of the state govern
ments, between the Congress and the people, to execute any
one power vested in the general government, and that the
constitution and laws of every state are nullified and declared
void, so far as they are or shall be inconsistent with this constitution, or the laws made in pursuance of it, or with treaties
made under the authority of the United States.—The government then, so far as it extends, is a complete one, and not a
confederation. It is as much one complete government as that
of New-York or Massachusetts, has as absolute and perfect
powers to make and execute all laws, to appoint officers, institute courts, declare offences, and annex penalties, with respect to every object to which it extends, as any other in the
world. So far therefore as its powers reach, all ideas of confederation are given up and lost. It is true this government is
limited to certain objects, or to speak more properly, some
small degree of power is still left to the states, but a little attention to the powers vested in the general government, will
convince every candid man, that if it is capable of being executed, all that is reserved for the individual states must very
soon be annihilated, except so far as they are barely necessary
to the organization of the general government. The powers
of the general legislature extend to every case that is of the
least importance—there is nothing valuable to human nature, nothing dear to freemen, but what is within its power.
It has authority to make laws which will affect the lives, the
liberty, and property of every man in the United States; nor

can the constitution or laws of any state, in any way prevent or impede the full and complete execution of every power given. The legislative power is competent to lay taxes, duties, imposts, and excises;—there is no limitation to this power, unless it be said that the clause which directs the use to which those taxes, and duties shall be applied, may be said to be a limitation: but this is no restriction of the power at all, for by this clause they are to be applied to pay the debts and provide for the common defence and general welfare of the United States; but the legislature have authority to contract debts at their discretion; they are the sole judges of what is necessary to provide for the common defence, and they only are to determine what is for the general welfare; this power therefore is neither more nor less, than a power to lay and collect taxes, imposts, and excises, at their pleasure; not only [is] the power to lay taxes unlimited, as to the amount they may require, but it is perfect and absolute to raise them in any mode they please. No state legislature, or any power in the state governments, have any more to do in carrying this into effect, than the authority of one state has to do with that of another. In the business therefore of laying and collecting taxes, the idea of confederation is totally lost, and that of one entire republic is embraced. It is proper here to remark, that the authority to lay and collect taxes is the most important of any power that can be granted; it connects with it almost all other powers, or at least will in process of time draw all other after it; it is the great mean of protection, security, and defence, in a good government, and the great engine of oppression and tyranny in a bad one. This cannot fail of being the case, if we consider the contracted limits which are set by this constitution, to the late [state?] governments, on this article of raising money. No state can emit paper money—lay any duties, or imposts, on imports, or exports, but by consent of the Congress; and then the net produce shall be for the benefit of the United States: the only mean therefore left, for any state to support its government and discharge its debts, is by direct taxation; and the United States have also power to lay and collect taxes, in any way they please. Every one who has thought on the subject, must be convinced that but small sums of money can be collected in any country, by direct taxe[s], when the federal government begins to exercise the right of taxation in all its parts, the legislatures of the several states will find it impossible to raise monies to support their governments. Without money they cannot be supported, and they must dwindle away, and, as before observed, their powers absorbed in that of the general government.

It might be here shown, that the power in the federal legislative, to raise and support armies at pleasure, as well in peace as in war, and their control over the militia, tend, not only to a consolidation of the government, but the destruction of liberty.—I shall not, however, dwell upon these, as a few observations upon the judicial power of this government, in addition to the preceding, will fully evince the truth of the position.

The judicial power of the United States is to be vested in a supreme court, and in such inferior courts as Congress may from time to time ordain and establish. The powers of these courts are very extensive; their jurisdiction comprehends all civil causes, except such as arise between citizens of the same state; and it extends to all cases in law and equity arising under the constitution. One inferior court must be established, I presume, in each state, at least, with the necessary executive officers appendant thereto. It is easy to see, that in the common course of things, these courts will eclipse the dignity, and take away from the respectability, of the state courts. These courts will be, in themselves, totally independent of the states, deriving their authority from the United States, and receiving from them fixed salaries; and in the course of human events it is to be expected, that they will swallow up all the powers of the courts in the respective states.

How far the clause in the 8th section of the 1st article may operate to do away all idea of confederated states, and to effect an entire consolidation of the whole into one general government, it is impossible to say. The powers given by this article are very general and comprehensive, and it may receive a construction to justify the passing almost any law. A power to make all laws, which shall be necessary and proper, for carrying into execution, all powers vested by the constitution in the government of the United States, or any department or officer thereof, is a power very comprehensive and definite [indefinite?], and may, for ought I know, be exercised in a such manner as entirely to abolish the state legislatures. Suppose the legislature of a state should pass a law to raise money to support their government and pay the state debt, may the Congress repeal this law, because it may prevent the collection of a tax which they may think proper and necessary to lay, to provide for the general welfare of the United States? For all laws made, in pursuance of this constitution, are the supreme law of the land, and the judges in every state shall be bound thereby, any thing in the constitution or laws of the different states to the contrary notwithstanding.—By such a law, the government of a particular state might be overturned at one stroke, and thereby be deprived of every means of its support.

It is not meant, by stating this case, to insinuate that the constitution would warrant a law of this kind; or unnecessarily to alarm the fears of the people, by suggesting, that the federal legislature would be more likely to pass the limits assigned them by the constitution, than that of an individual state, further than they are less responsible to the people. But what is meant is, that the legislature of the United States are vested with the great and uncontrollable powers, of laying and collecting taxes, duties, imposts, and excises: of regulating trade, raising and supporting armies, organizing, arming, and disciplining the militia, instituting courts, and other general powers. And are by this clause invested with the power of making all laws, proper and necessary, for carrying all these into execution; and they may so exercise this power as entirely to annihilate all the state governments, and reduce this country to one single government. And if they may do it, it is pretty certain they will; for it will be found that the power retained by individual states, small as it is, will be a clog upon the wheels of the government of the United States; the latter therefore will be naturally inclined to remove it out of the way. Besides, it is a truth confirmed by the unerring experience of ages, that every man, and every body of men, invested with power, are ever disposed to increase it, and to acquire a superiority over every thing that stands in their way. This disposition, which is implanted in human nature, will operate in the federal legislature to lessen and ultimately to subvert the state authority, and having such advantages, will most certainly succeed, if the federal government succeeds at all. It must be very evident then, that what this constitution wants of being a complete consolidation of the several parts of the union into one complete government, possessed of perfect legislative, judicial, and executive powers, to all intents and purposes, it will necessarily acquire in its exercise and operation.

The Federalist No. 9, by Alexander Hamilton (1787)

The utility of a confederacy, as well to suppress faction and to guard the internal tranquillity of States, as to increase their external force and security, is in reality not a new idea. It has been practiced upon in different countries and ages, and has received the sanction of the most applauded writers, on the subjects of politics. The opponents of the PLAN proposed have with great assiduity cited and circulated the observations of Montesquieu on the necessity of a contracted territory for a republican government. But they seem not to have been apprised of the sentiments of that great man expressed in another part of his work, nor to have adverted to the consequences of the principle to which they subscribe, with such ready acquiescence.

When Montesquieu recommends a small extent for republics, the standards he had in view were of dimensions, far short of the limits of almost every one of these States. Neither Virginia, Massachusetts, Pennsylvania, New-York, North-Carolina, nor Georgia, can by any means be compared with the models, from which he reasoned and to which the terms of his description apply. If we therefore take his ideas on this point, as the criterion of truth, we shall be driven to the alternative, either of taking refuge at once in the arms of monarchy, or of splitting ourselves into an infinity of little jealous, clashing, tumultuous commonwealths, the wretched nurseries of unceasing discord and the miserable objects of universal pity or contempt. Some of the writers, who have come forward on the other side of the question, seem to have been aware of the dilemma; and have even been bold enough to hint at the division of the larger States, as a desirable thing. Such an infatuated policy, such a desperate expedient, might, by the multiplication of petty offices, answer the views of men, who possess not qualifications to extend their influence beyond the narrow circles of personal intrigue, but it could never promote the greatness or happiness of the people of America.

Referring the examination of the principle itself to another place, as has been already mentioned, it will be sufficient to remark here, that in the sense of the author who has been most emphatically quoted upon the occasion, it would only dictate a reduction of the SIZE of the more considerable MEMBERS of the Union; but would not militate against their being all comprehended in one Confederate Government. And this is the true question, in the discussion of which we are at present interested.

So far are the suggestions of Montesquieu from standing in opposition to a general Union of the States, that he explicitly treats of a CONFEDERATE REPUBLIC as the expedient for extending the sphere of popular government and reconciling the advantages of monarchy with those of republicanism.

"It is very probable" (says he) "that mankind would have been obliged, at length, to live constantly under the government of a SINGLE PERSON, had they not contrived a kind of constitution, that has all the internal advantages of a republican, together with the external force of a monarchial government. I mean a CONFEDERATE REPUBLIC.

"This form of Government is a Convention, by which several smaller States agree to become members of a larger one, which they intend to form. It is a kind of assemblage of societies, that constitute a new one, capable of increasing, by means of new associations, till they arrive to such a degree of power as to be able to provide for the security of the united body.

"A republic of this kind, able to withstand an external force, may support itself without any internal corruption. The form of this society prevents all manner of inconveniencies.

"If a single member should attempt to usurp the supreme authority, he could not be supposed to have an equal authority and credit, in all the confederate states. Were he to have too great influence over one, this would alarm the rest. Were he to subdue a part, that which would still remain free might oppose him with forces, independent of those which he had usurped, and overpower him before he could be settled in his usurpation.

"Should a popular insurrection happen, in one of the confederate States, the others are able to quell it. Should abuses creep into one part, they are reformed by those that remain sound. The State may be destroyed on one side, and not on the other; the confederacy may be dissolved, and the confederates preserve their sovereignty.

"As this government is composed of small republics it enjoys the internal happiness of each, and with respect to its external situation it is possessed, by means of the association of all the advantages of large monarchies."

I have thought it proper to quote at length these interesting passages, because they contain a luminous abridgment of the principal arguments in favor of the Union, and must effectually remove the false impressions, which a misapplication of other parts of the work was calculated to produce. They have at the same time an intimate connection with the more immediate design of this Paper; which is to illustrate the tendency of the Union to repress domestic faction and insurrection.

A distinction, more subtle than accurate has been raised between a confederacy and a consolidation of the States. The essential characteristic of the first is said to be, the restriction of its authority to the members in their collective capacities, without reaching to the individuals of whom they are composed. It is contended that the national council ought to have no concern with any object of internal administration. An exact equality of suffrage between the members has also been insisted upon as a leading feature of a Confederate Government. These positions are in the main arbitrary; they are supported neither by principle nor precedent. It has indeed happened that governments of this kind have generally operated in the manner, which the distinction, taken notice of, supposes to be inherent in their nature—but there have been in most of them extensive exceptions to the practice, which serve to prove as far as example will go, that there is no absolute rule on the subject. And it will be clearly shewn, in the course of this investigation, that as far as the principle contended for has prevailed, it has been the cause of incurable disorder and imbecility in the government.

The definition of a Confederate Republic seems simply to be, an "assemblage of societies" or an association of two or more States into one State. The extent, modifications and objects of the Federal authority are mere matters of discretion. So long as the separate organization of the members be not abolished, so long as it exists by a constitutional necessity for local purposes, though it should be in perfect subordination to the general authority of the Union, it would still be, in fact and in theory, an association of States, or a confederacy. The proposed Constitution, so far from implying an abolition of the State Governments, makes them constituent parts of the national sovereignty by allowing them a direct representation in the Senate, and leaves in their possession certain exclusive and very important portions of sovereign power. This fully corresponds, in every rational import of the terms, with the idea of a Federal Government.

Brutus No. 2
(1787)

Though it should be admitted, that the argument[s] against reducing all the states into one consolidated government, are not sufficient fully to establish this point; yet they will, at least, justify this conclusion, that in forming a constitution for such a country, great care should be taken to limit and definite its powers, adjust its parts, and guard against an abuse of authority. How far attention has been paid to these objects, shall be the subject of future enquiry. When a building is to be erected which is intended to stand for ages, the foundation should be firmly laid. The constitution proposed to your acceptance, is designed not for yourselves alone, but for generations yet unborn. The principles, therefore, upon which the social compact is founded, ought to have been clearly and precisely stated, and the most express and full declaration of rights to have been made—But on this subject there is almost an entire silence.

If we may collect the sentiments of the people of America, from their own most solemn declarations, they hold this truth as self-evident, that all men are by nature free. No one man, therefore, or any class of men, have a right, by the law of nature, or of God, to assume or exercise authority over their fellows. The origin of society then is to be sought, not in any natural right which one man has to exercise authority over another, but in the united consent of those who associate. The mutual wants of men, at first dictated the propriety of forming societies; and when they were established, protection and defense pointed out the necessity of instituting government. In a state of nature every individual pursues his own interest; in this pursuit it frequently happened, that the possessions or enjoyments of one were sacrificed to the views and designs of another; thus the weak were a prey to the strong, the simple and unwary were subject to impositions from those who were more crafty and designing. In this state of things, every individual was insecure; common interest therefore directed, that government should be established, in which the force of the whole community should be collected, and under such directions, as to protect and defend every one who composed it. The common good, therefore, is the end of civil government, and common consent, the foundation on which it is established. To effect this end, it was necessary that a certain portion of natural liberty should be surrendered, in order, that what remained should be preserved: how great a proportion of natural freedom is necessary to be yielded by individuals, when they submit to government, I shall not now enquire. So much, however, must be given up, as will be sufficient to enable those, to whom the administration of the government is committed, to establish laws for the promoting the happiness of the community, and to carry those laws into effect. But it is not necessary, for this purpose, that individuals should relinquish all their natural rights. Some are of such a nature that they cannot be surrendered. Of this kind are the rights of conscience, the right of enjoying and defending life, etc. Others are not necessary to be resigned, in order to attain the end for which government is instituted, these therefore ought not to be given up. To surrender them, would counteract the very end of government, to wit, the common good. From these observations it appears, that in forming a government on its true principles, the foundation should be laid in the manner I before stated, by expressly reserving to the people such of their essential natural rights, as are not necessary to be parted with. The same reasons which at first induced mankind to associate and institute government, will operate to influence them to observe this precaution. If they had been disposed to conform themselves to the rule of immutable righteousness, government would not have been requisite. It was because one part exercised fraud, oppression, and violence on the other, that men came together, and agreed that certain rules should be formed, to regulate the conduct of all, and the power of the whole community lodged in the hands of rulers to enforce an obedience to them. But rulers have the same propensities as other men; they are as likely to use the power with which they are vested for private purposes, and to the injury and oppression of those over whom they are placed, as individuals in a state of nature are to injure and oppress one another. It is therefore as proper that bounds should be set to their authority, as that government should have at first been instituted to restrain private injuries.

This principle, which seems so evidently founded in the reason and nature of things, is confirmed by universal experience. Those who have governed, have been found in all ages ever active to enlarge their powers and abridge the public liberty. This has induced the people in all countries, where any sense of freedom remained, to fix barriers against the encroachments of their rulers. The country from which we have derived our origin, is an eminent example of this. Their Magna Charta and Bill of Rights have long been the boast, as well as the security, of that nation. I need say no more, I presume, to an American, than, that this principle is a fundamental one, in all the constitutions of our own states; there is not one of them but what is either founded on a declaration or bill of rights, or has certain express reservation of rights interwoven in the body of them. From this it appears, that at a time when the pulse of liberty beat high and when an appeal was made to the people to form constitutions for the government of themselves, it was their universal sense, that such declarations should make a part of their frames of government. It is therefore the more astonishing, that this grand security, to the rights of the people, is not to be found in this Constitution.

It has been said, in answer to this objection, that such declaration[s] of rights, however requisite they might be in the constitutions of the states, are not necessary in the general Constitution, because, "in the former case, every thing which is not reserved is given, but in the latter the reverse of the proposition prevails, and every thing which is not given is reserved." It requires but little attention to discover, that this mode of reasoning is rather specious than solid. The powers, rights, and authority, granted to the general government by this constitution, are as complete, with respect to every object to which they extend, as that of any state government—It reaches to every thing which concerns human happiness—Life, liberty, and property, are under its control. There is the same reason, therefore, that the exercise of power, in this case, should be restrained within proper limits, as in that of the state governments. To set this matter in a clear light, permit me to instance some of the articles of the bills of rights of the individual states, and apply them to the case in question.

For the security of life, in criminal prosecutions, the bills of rights of most of the states have declared, that no man shall be held to answer for a crime until he is made fully acquainted with the charge brought against him; he shall not be compelled to accuse, or furnish evidence against himself—The witnesses against him shall be brought face to face, and he shall be fully heard by himself or counsel. That it is essential to the security of life and liberty, that trial of facts be in the vicinity where they happen. Are not provisions of this kind as necessary in the general government, as in that of a particular state? The powers vested in the new Congress extend in many cases to life; they are authorized to provide for the punishment of a variety of capital crimes, and no restraint is laid upon them in its exercise, save only, that "the trial of all crimes, except in cases of impeachment, shall be by jury; and such trial shall be in the state where the said crimes shall have been committed." No man is secure of a trial in the county where he is charged to have committed a crime; he may be brought from Niagara to New York, or carried from Kentucky to Richmond for trial for an offence, supposed to be committed. What security is there, that a man shall be furnished with a full and plain description of the charges against him? That he shall be allowed to produce all proof he can in his favor? That he shall see the witnesses against him face to face, or that he shall be fully heard in his own defense by himself or counsel?

For the security of liberty it has been declared, "that excessive bail should not be required, nor excessive fines imposed, nor cruel or unusual punishments inflicted—That all warrants, without oath or affirmation, to search suspected places, or seize any person, his papers or property, are grievous and oppressive."

These provisions are as necessary under the general government as under that of the individual states; for the power of the former is as complete to the purpose of requiring bail, imposing fines, inflicting punishments, granting search warrants, and seizing persons, papers, or property, in certain cases, as the other.

For the purpose of securing the property of the citizens,

it is declared by all the states, "that in all controversies at law, respecting property, the ancient mode of trial by jury is one of the best securities of the rights of the people, and ought to remain sacred and inviolable."

Does not the same necessity exist of reserving this right, under this national compact, as in that of these states? Yet nothing is said respecting it. In the bills of rights of the states it is declared, that a well regulated militia is the proper and natural defense of a free government—That as standing armies in time of peace are dangerous, they are not to be kept up, and that the military should be kept under strict subordination to, and controlled by the civil power.

The same security is as necessary in this Constitution, and much more so; for the general government will have the sole power to raise and to pay armies, and are under no control in the exercise of it; yet nothing of this is to be found in this new system.

I might proceed to instance a number of other rights, which were as necessary to be reserved, such as, that elections should be free, that the liberty of the press should be held sacred; but the instances adduced, are sufficient to prove, that this argument is without foundation.—Besides, it is evident, that the reason here assigned was not the true one, why the framers of this constitution omitted a bill of rights; if it had been, they would not have made certain reservations, while they totally omitted others of more importance. We find they have, in the 9th section of the 1st article, declared, that the writ of habeas corpus shall not be suspended, unless in cases of rebellion—that no bill of attainder, or ex-post facto law, shall be passed—that no title of nobility shall be granted by the United States, &c. If every thing which is not given is reserved, what propriety is there in these exceptions? Does this constitution any where grant the power of suspending the habeas corpus, to make ex-post facto laws, pass bills of attainder, or grant titles of nobility? It certainly does not in express terms. The only answer that can be given is, that these are implied in the general powers granted. With equal truth it may be said, that all the powers, which the bills of right guard against the abuse of, are contained or implied in the general ones granted by this constitution.

So far it is from being true, that a bill of rights is less necessary in the general constitution than in those of the states, the contrary is evidently the fact.—This system, if it is possible for the people of America to accede to it, will be an original compact; and being the last, will, in the nature of things, vacate every former agreement inconsistent with it. For it being a plan of government received and ratified by the whole people, all other forms, which are in existence at the time of its adoption, must yield to it. This is expressed in positive and unequivocal terms, in the 6th article, "That this constitution and the laws of the United States, which shall be made in pursuance thereof, and all treaties made, or which shall be made, under the authority of the United States, shall be the supreme law of the land; and the judges in every state shall be bound thereby, any thing in the constitution, or laws of any state, to the contrary notwithstanding.

"The senators and representatives before mentioned, and the members of the several state legislatures, and all executive and judicial officers, both of the United States, and of the several states, shall be bound, by oath or affirmation, to support this constitution."

It is therefore not only necessarily implied thereby, but positively expressed, that the different state constitutions are repealed and entirely done away, so far as they are inconsistent with this, with the laws which shall be made in pursuance thereof, or with treaties made, or which shall be made, under the authority of the United States; of what avail will the constitutions of the respective states be to preserve the rights of its citizens? should they be plead, the answer would be, the constitution of the United States, and the laws made in pursuance thereof, is the supreme law, and all legislatures and judicial officers, whether of the general or state governments, are bound by oath to support it. No privilege, reserved by the bills of rights, or secured by the state government, can limit the power granted by this, or restrain any laws made in pursuance of it. It stands therefore on its own bottom, and must receive a construction by itself without any reference to any other—and hence it was of the highest importance, that the most precise and express declarations and reservations of rights should have been made.

This will appear the more necessary, when it is considered, that not only the Constitution and laws made in pursuance thereof, but all treaties made, or which shall be made, under the authority of the United States, are the supreme law of the land, and supersede the constitutions of all the states. The power to make treaties, is vested in the president, by and with the advice and consent of two thirds of the senate. I do not find any limitation, or restriction, to the exercise of this power. The most important article in any constitution may therefore be repealed, even without a legislative act. Ought not a government, vested with such extensive and indefinite authority, to have been restricted by a declaration of rights? It certainly ought.

So clear a point is this, that I cannot help suspecting, that persons who attempt to persuade people, that such reservations were less necessary under this Constitution than under those of the states, are willfully endeavoring to deceive, and to lead you into an absolute state of vassalage.

The Federalist No. 84, by Alexander Hamilton (1788)

The most considerable of these remaining objections is, that the plan of the convention contains no bill of rights. Among other answers given to this, it has been upon different occasions remarked, that the constitutions of several of the states are in a similar predicament. I add, that New-York is of this number. And yet the opposers of the new system in this state, who profess an unlimited admiration for its constitution, are among the most intemperate partizans of a bill of rights. To justify their zeal in this matter, they alledge two things; one is, that though the constitution of New-York has no bill of rights prefixed to it, yet it contains in the body of it various provisions in favour of particular privileges and rights, which in substance amount to the same thing; the other is, that the constitution adopts in their full extent the common and statute law of Great-Britain, by which many other rights not expressed in it are equally secured.

To the first I answer, that the constitution proposed by the convention contains, as well as the constitution of this state, a number of such provisions.

Independent of those, which relate to the structure of the government, we find the following: Article I. section 3. clause 7. "Judgment in cases of impeachment shall not extend further than to removal from office, and disqualification to hold and enjoy any office of honour, trust or profit under the United States; but the party convicted shall nevertheless be liable and subject to indictment, trial, judgment and punishment, according to law." Section 9. of the same article, clause 2. "The privilege of the writ of habeas corpus shall not be suspended, unless when in cases of rebellion or invasion the public safety may require it." Clause 3. "No bill of attainder or ex post facto law shall be passed." Clause [8]. "No title of nobility shall be granted by the United States: And no person holding any office of profit or trust under them, shall, without the consent of the congress, accept of any present, emolument, office or title, of any kind whatever, from any king, prince or foreign state." Article III. section 2. clause 3. "The trial of all crimes, except in cases of impeachment, shall be by jury; and such trial shall be held in the state where the said crimes shall have been committed; but when not committed within any state, the trial shall be at such place or places as the congress may by law have directed." Section 3, of the same article, "Treason against the United States shall consist only in levying war against them, or in adhering to their enemies, giving them aid and comfort. No person shall be convicted of treason unless on the testimony of two witnesses to the same overt act, or on confession in open court." And clause [2], of the same section. "The congress shall have power to declare the punishment of treason, but no attainder of treason shall work corruption of blood, or forfeiture, except during the life of the person attainted."

It may well be a question whether these are not upon the whole, of equal importance with any which are to be found in the constitution of this state. The establishment of the writ of habeas corpus, the prohibition of ex post facto laws, and of TITLES OF NOBILITY, to which we have no corresponding provisions in our constitution, are perhaps greater securities to liberty and republicanism than any it contains. The creation of crimes after the commission of the fact, or in other words, the subjecting of men to punishment for things which, when they were done, were breaches of no law, and the practice of arbitrary imprisonments have been in all ages the favourite and most formidable instruments of tyranny. The observations of the judicious Blackstone in reference to the latter, are well worthy of recital. "To bereave a man of life (says he) or by violence to confiscate his estate, without accusation or trial, would be so gross and notorious an act of despotism, as must at once convey the alarm of tyranny throughout the whole nation; but confinement of the person by secretly hurrying him to gaol, where his sufferings are unknown or forgotten, is a less public, a less striking, and therefore a more dangerous engine of arbitrary government." And as a remedy for this fatal evil, he is every where peculiarly emphatical in his encomiums on the habeas corpus act, which in one place he calls "the BULWARK of the British constitution."

Nothing need be said to illustrate the importance of the prohibition of titles of nobility. This may truly be denominated the corner stone of republican government; for so long as they are excluded, there can never be serious danger that the government will be any other than that of the people.

To the second, that is, to the pretended establishment of the common and statute law by the constitution, I answer, that they are expressly made subject "to such alterations and provisions as the legislature shall from time to time make concerning the same." They are therefore at any moment liable to repeal by the ordinary legislative power, and of course have no constitutional sanction. The only use of the declaration was to recognize the ancient law, and to remove doubts which might have been occasioned by the revolution. This consequently can be considered as no part of a declaration of rights, which under our constitutions must be intended as limitations of the power of the government itself.

It has been several times truly remarked, that bills of rights are in their origin, stipulations between kings and their subjects, abridgments of prerogative in favor of privilege, reservations of rights not surrendered to the prince. Such was Magna Charta, obtained by the Barons, sword in hand, from king John. Such were the subsequent confirmations of that charter by subsequent princes. Such was the petition of right assented to by Charles the First, in the beginning of his reign. Such also was the declaration of right presented by the lords and commons to the prince of Orange in 1688, and afterwards thrown into the form of an act of parliament, called the bill of rights. It is evident, therefore, that according to their primitive signification, they have no application to constitutions professedly founded upon the power of the people, and executed by their immediate representatives and servants. Here, in strictness, the people surrender nothing, and as they retain every thing, they have no need of particular reservations. "We the people of the United States, to secure the blessings of liberty to ourselves and our posterity, do ordain and establish this constitution for the United States of America." Here is a better recognition of popular rights than volumes of those aphorisms which make the principal figure in several of our state bills of rights, and which would sound much better in a treatise of ethics than in a constitution of government.

But a minute detail of particular rights is certainly far less applicable to a constitution like that under consideration, which is merely intended to regulate the general political interests of the nation, than to a constitution which has the regulation of every species of personal and private concerns. If therefore the loud clamours against the plan of the convention on this score, are well founded, no epithets of reprobation will be too strong for the constitution of this state. But the truth is, that both of them contain all, which in relation to their objects, is reasonably to be desired.

I go further, and affirm that bills of rights, in the sense and in the extent in which they are contended for, are not only unnecessary in the proposed constitution, but would even be dangerous. They would contain various exceptions to powers which are not granted; and on this very account, would afford a colorable pretext to claim more than were granted. For why declare that things shall not be done which there is no power to do? Why for instance, should it be said, that the liberty of the press shall not be restrained, when no power is given by which restrictions may be imposed? I will not contend that such a provision would confer a regulating power; but it is evident that it would furnish, to men disposed to usurp, a plausible pretense for claiming that power. They might urge with a semblance of reason, that the constitution ought not to be charged with the absurdity of providing against the abuse of an authority, which was not given, and that the provision against restraining the liberty of the press afforded a clear implication, that a power to prescribe proper regulations concerning it, was intended to be vested in the national government. This may serve as a specimen of the numerous handles which would be given to the doctrine of constructive powers, by the indulgence of an injudicious zeal for bills of rights.

On the subject of the liberty of the press, as much has been said, I cannot forbear adding a remark or two: In the first place, I observe that there is not a syllable concerning it in the constitution of this state, and in the next, I contend that whatever has been said about it in that of any other state, amounts to nothing. What signifies a declaration that "the liberty of the press shall be inviolably preserved?" What is the liberty of the press? Who can give it any definition which would not leave the utmost latitude for evasion? I hold it to be impracticable; and from this, I infer, that its security, whatever fine declarations may be inserted in any constitution respecting it, must altogether depend on public opinion, and on the general spirit of the people and of the government. And here, after all, as intimated upon another occasion, must we seek for the only solid basis of all our rights.

There remains but one other view of this matter to conclude the point. The truth is, after all the declamation we have heard, that the constitution is itself in every rational sense, and to every useful purpose, A BILL OF RIGHTS. The several bills of rights, in Great-Britain, form its constitution, and conversely the constitution of each state is its bill of rights. And the proposed constitution, if adopted, will be the bill of rights of the union. Is it one object of a bill of rights to declare and specify the political privileges of the citizens in the structure and administration of the government? This is done in the most ample and precise manner in the plan of the convention, comprehending various precautions for the public security, which are not to be found in any of the state constitutions. Is another object of a bill of rights to define certain immunities and modes of proceeding, which are relative to personal and private concerns? This we have seen has also been attended to, in a variety of cases, in the same plan. Adverting therefore to the substantial meaning of a bill of rights, it is absurd to allege that it is not to be found in the work of the convention. It may be said that it does not go far enough, though it will not be easy to make this appear; but it can with no propriety be contended that there is no such thing. It certainly must be immaterial what mode is observed as to the order of declaring the rights of the citizens, if they are to be found in any part of the instrument which establishes the government. And hence it must be apparent that much of what has been said on this subject rests merely on verbal and nominal distinctions, which are entirely foreign from the substance of the thing.

HAMILTON V. GEORGE MASON

(Pardoning Powers)

Debate in Virginia Ratifying Convention (1788)

Mr. George Mason, animadverting on the magnitude of the powers of the President, was alarmed at the additional power of commanding the army in person. He admitted the propriety of his being commander-in-chief, so far as to give orders and have a general superintendency; but he thought it would be dangerous to let him command in person, without any restraint, as he might make a bad use of it. He was, then, clearly of opinion that the consent of a majority of both houses of Congress should be required before he could take the command in person. If at any time it should be necessary that he should take the personal command, either on account of his superior abilities or other cause, then Congress would agree to it; and all dangers would be obviated by requiring their consent. He called to gentlemen's recollection the extent of what the late commander-in-chief might have done, from his great abilities, and the strong attachment of both officers and soldiers towards him, if, instead of being disinterested, he had been an ambitious man. So disinterested and amiable a character as General Washington might never command again. The possibility of danger ought to be guarded against.

Although he did not disapprove of the President's consultation with the principle executive officers, yet he objected to the want of an executive council, which he conceived to be necessary to any regular free government. There being none such, he apprehended a council would arise out of the Senate, which, for want of real responsibility, he thought dangerous. You will please, says he, to recollect that removal from office, and future disqualification to hold any office, are the only consequences of conviction on impeachment. Now, I conceive that the President ought not to have the power of pardoning, because he may frequently pardon crimes which were advised by himself. It may happen, at some future day, that he will establish a monarchy, and destroy the republic. If he has the power of granting pardons before indictment, or conviction, may he not stop inquiry and prevent detection? The case of treason ought, at least, to be excepted. This is a weighty objection with me.

The Federalist Papers, No. 69, by Alexander Hamilton (1788)

To the People of the State of New York:

I PROCEED now to trace the real characters of the proposed Executive, as they are marked out in the plan of the convention. This will serve to place in a strong light the unfairness of the representations which have been made in regard to it.

The first thing which strikes our attention is, that the executive authority, with few exceptions, is to be vested in a single magistrate. This will scarcely, however, be considered as a point upon which any comparison can be grounded; for if, in this particular, there be a resemblance to the king of Great Britain, there is not less a resemblance to the Grand Seignior, to the khan of Tartary, to the Man of the Seven Mountains, or to the governor of New York.

That magistrate is to be elected for FOUR years; and is to be re-eligible as often as the people of the United States shall think him worthy of their confidence. In these circumstances there is a total dissimilitude between HIM and a king of Great Britain, who is an HEREDITARY monarch, possessing the crown as a patrimony descendible to his heirs forever; but there is a close analogy between HIM and a governor of New York, who is elected for THREE years, and is re-eligible without limitation or intermission. If we consider how much

less time would be requisite for establishing a dangerous influence in a single State, than for establishing a like influence
throughout the United States, we must conclude that a duration of FOUR years for the Chief Magistrate of the Union is
a degree of permanency far less to be dreaded in that office,
than a duration of THREE years for a corresponding office
in a single State.

The President of the United States would be liable to be
impeached, tried, and, upon conviction of treason, bribery,
or other high crimes or misdemeanors, removed from office;
and would afterwards be liable to prosecution and punishment in the ordinary course of law. The person of the king of
Great Britain is sacred and inviolable; there is no constitutional
tribunal to which he is amenable; no punishment to which he
can be subjected without involving the crisis of a national
revolution. In this delicate and important circumstance of
personal responsibility, the President of Confederated America would stand upon no better ground than a governor of
New York, and upon worse ground than the governors of
Maryland and Delaware.

The President of the United States is to have power to return a bill, which shall have passed the two branches of the
legislature, for reconsideration; and the bill so returned is to
become a law, if, upon that reconsideration, it be approved by
two thirds of both houses. The king of Great Britain, on his
part, has an absolute negative upon the acts of the two houses
of Parliament. The disuse of that power for a considerable time
past does not affect the reality of its existence; and is to be
ascribed wholly to the crown's having found the means of
substituting influence to authority, or the art of gaining a majority in one or the other of the two houses, to the necessity
of exerting a prerogative which could seldom be exerted without hazarding some degree of national agitation. The quali-

fied negative of the President differs widely from this absolute negative of the British sovereign; and tallies exactly with the revisionary authority of the council of revision of this State, of which the governor is a constituent part. In this respect the power of the President would exceed that of the governor of New York, because the former would possess, singly, what the latter shares with the chancellor and judges; but it would be precisely the same with that of the governor of Massachusetts, whose constitution, as to this article, seems to have been the original from which the convention have copied.

The President is to be the "commander-in-chief of the army and navy of the United States, and of the militia of the several States, when called into the actual service of the United States. He is to have power to grant reprieves and pardons for offenses against the United States, EXCEPT IN CASES OF IMPEACHMENT; to recommend to the consideration of Congress such measures as he shall judge necessary and expedient; to convene, on extraordinary occasions, both houses of the legislature, or either of them, and, in case of disagreement between them WITH RESPECT TO THE TIME OF ADJOURNMENT, to adjourn them to such time as he shall think proper; to take care that the laws be faithfully executed; and to commission all officers of the United States." In most of these particulars, the power of the President will resemble equally that of the king of Great Britain and of the governor of New York. The most material points of difference are these:

First. The President will have only the occasional command of such part of the militia of the nation as by legislative provision may be called into the actual service of the Union. The king of Great Britain and the governor of New York have at all times the entire command of all the militia within their several jurisdictions. In this article, therefore, the power of the President would be inferior to that of either the monarch or the governor.

Secondly. The President is to be commander-in-chief of the army and navy of the United States. In this respect his authority would be nominally the same with that of the king of Great Britain, but in substance much inferior to it. It would amount to nothing more than the supreme command and direction of the military and naval forces, as first General and admiral of the Confederacy; while that of the British king extends to the DECLARING of war and to the RAISING and REGULATING of fleets and armies, all which, by the Constitution under consideration, would appertain to the legislature. The governor of New York, on the other hand, is by the constitution of the State vested only with the command of its militia and navy. But the constitutions of several of the States expressly declare their governors to be commanders-in-chief, as well of the army as navy; and it may well be a question, whether those of New Hampshire and Massachusetts, in particular, do not, in this instance, confer larger powers upon their respective governors, than could be claimed by a President of the United States.

Thirdly. The power of the President, in respect to pardons, would extend to all cases, EXCEPT THOSE OF IMPEACHMENT. The governor of New York may pardon in all cases, even in those of impeachment, except for treason and murder. Is not the power of the governor, in this article, on a calculation of political consequences, greater than that of the President? All conspiracies and plots against the government, which have not been matured into actual treason, may be screened from punishment of every kind, by the interposition of the prerogative of pardoning. If a governor of New York, therefore, should be at the head of any such conspiracy, until the design had been ripened into actual hostility he could insure his accomplices and adherents an entire impunity. A President of the Union, on the other hand, though he may even pardon treason, when prosecuted in the ordinary course of law, could shelter no offender, in any degree, from the effects of impeachment and conviction. Would not the prospect of a total indemnity for all the preliminary steps be a greater temptation to undertake and persevere in an enterprise against the public liberty, than the mere prospect of an exemption from death and confiscation, if the final execution of the design, upon an actual appeal to arms, should miscarry? Would this last expectation have any influence at all, when the probability was computed, that the person who was to afford that exemption might himself be involved in the consequences of the measure, and might be incapacitated by his agency in it from affording the desired impunity? The better to judge of this matter, it will be necessary to recollect, that, by the proposed Constitution, the offense of treason is limited "to levying war upon the United States, and adhering to their enemies, giving them aid and comfort"; and that by the laws of New York it is confined within similar bounds. . . .

The President of the United States would be an officer elected by the people for FOUR years; the king of Great Britain is a perpetual and HEREDITARY prince. The one would be amenable to personal punishment and disgrace; the person of the other is sacred and inviolable. The one would have a QUALIFIED negative upon the acts of the legislative body; the other has an ABSOLUTE negative. The one would have a right to command the military and naval forces of the nation; the other, in addition to this right, possesses that of DECLARING war, and of RAISING and REGULATING fleets and armies by his own authority. The one would have a concurrent power with a branch of the legislature in the formation of treaties; the other is the SOLE POSSESSOR of the power of making treaties. The one would have a like concurrent authority in appointing to offices; the other is the sole author of all appointments. The one can confer no privileges whatever; the other can make denizens of aliens, noblemen of commoners; can erect corporations with all the rights incident to corporate bodies. The one can prescribe no rules concerning the commerce or currency of the nation; the other is in several respects the arbiter of commerce, and in this capacity can establish markets and fairs, can regulate weights and measures, can lay embargoes for a limited time, can coin money, can authorize or prohibit the circulation of foreign coin. The one has no particle of spiritual jurisdiction; the other is the supreme head and governor of the national church! What answer shall we give to those who would persuade us that things so unlike resemble each other? The same that ought to be given to those who tell us that a government, the whole power of which would be in the hands of the elective and periodical servants of the people, is an aristocracy, a monarchy, and a despotism.

PUBLIUS.

Part III

DOES A STRONG GOVERNMENT USURP FREEDOM?

———— ☆ ————

*The Debates over
the Bank of the United States
and the War Powers*

Alexander Hamilton and James Madison were allies during the fight for ratification, and collaborators on The Federalist. But they soon became adversaries in the first presidential administration of George Washington. Hamilton saw the establishment of a bank of the United States as central to his understanding that a strong federal government was needed to create a free and stable society. However, in the proposal for the bank, both Madison and his ally, Secretary of State Thomas Jefferson, saw a threat to liberty—a vastly powerful federal government that could usurp the freedom best provided by local and state governments.

That same theme—and the same opposition among former friends—continued as Hamilton and Madison debated the role of the American presidency. For Hamilton, central-izing the war powers in the office of the president offered the best protection for American security. For Madison, a presi-dent who refused to defer to Congress on plans for neutrality or war risked the very tyranny the Constitution was designed to prevent.

The two debates in this section are different in topic, but parallel each other on the question of whether a strong fed-eral government is a threat to liberty or a necessity to se-cure it.

HAMILTON V. JAMES MADISON AND THOMAS JEFFERSON

(*Bank of the United States*)

"The Bank Bill," by James Madison (1791)

Mr. Madison began with a general review of the advantages and disadvantages of banks. The former he stated to consist in, first, the aids they afford to merchants who can thereby push their mercantile operations farther with the same capital. The aids to merchants in paying punctually the customs. Aids to the government in complying punctually with its engagements, when deficiencies or delays happen in the revenue. In diminishing usury. In saving the wear of the gold and silver kept in the vaults, and represented by notes. In facilitating occasional remittances from different places where notes happen to circulate. . . .

The principal disadvantages consisted in, banishing the precious metals, by substituting another medium to perform their office: This effect was inevitable. It was admitted by the most enlightened patrons of banks, particularly by Smith on the Wealth of Nations. The common answer to the objection was, that the money banished was only an exchange for something equally valuable that would be imported in return. He admitted the weight of this observation in general, but doubted whether, in the present habits of this country, the returns would not be in articles of no permanent use to it. Exposing the public and individuals to all the evils of a run on the bank, which would be particularly calamitous in so great a country as this, and might happen from various causes, as false rumours, bad management of the institution, an unfavorable balance of trade from short crops.

It was proper to be considered also, that the most important of the advantages would be better obtained by several banks properly distributed, than by a single one. The aids to commerce could only be afforded at or very near the seat of the bank. The same was true of aids to merchants in the payment of customs. Anticipations of the government would also be most convenient at the different places where the interest of the debt was to be paid. The case in America was different from that in England: the interest there was all due at one place, and the genius of the monarchy favored the concentration of wealth and influence at the metropolis.

He thought the plan liable to other objections: It did not make so good a bargain for the public as was due to its interests. The charter to the bank of England had been granted for 11 years only, and was paid for by a loan to the government on terms better than could be elsewhere got. Every renewal of the charter had in like manner been purchased; in some instances, at a very high price. The same had been done by the banks of Genoa, Naples, and other like banks of circulation. The plan was unequal to the public creditors—it gave an undue preference to the holders of a particular denomination of the public debt, and to those at and within reach of the seat of government. If the subscriptions should be rapid, the distant holders of paper would be excluded altogether.

In making these remarks on the merits of the bill, he had reserved to himself, he said, the right to deny the authority of Congress to pass it. He had entertained this opinion from the date of the constitution. His impression might perhaps be the stronger, because he well recollected that a power to grant charters of incorporation had been proposed in the general convention and rejected.

Is the power of establishing an *incorporated bank* among the powers vested by the constitution in the legislature of the United States? This is the question to be examined.

After some general remarks on the limitations of all political power, he took notice of the peculiar manner in which the federal government is limited. It is not a general grant, out of which particular powers are excepted—it is a grant of particular powers only, leaving the general mass in other hands. So it had been understood by its friends and its foes, and so it was to be interpreted.

As preliminaries to a right interpretation, he laid down the following rules:

An interpretation that destroys the very characteristic of the government cannot be just.

Where a meaning is clear, the consequences, whatever they may be, are to be admitted—where doubtful, it is fairly triable by its consequences. . . .

Reviewing the constitution with an eye to these positions, it was not possible to discover in it the power to incorporate a Bank. The only clauses under which such a power could be pretended, are either—

1. The power to lay and collect taxes to pay the debts, and provide for the common defence and general welfare: Or,

2. The power to borrow money on the credit of the United States: Or,

3. The power to pass all laws necessary and proper to carry into execution those powers.

The bill did not come within the first power. It laid no tax to pay the debts, or provide for the general welfare. It laid no tax whatever. It was altogether foreign to the subject.

No argument could be drawn from the terms "common defence, and general welfare." The power as to these general purposes, was limited to acts laying taxes for them; and the general purposes themselves were limited and explained by the particular enumeration subjoined. To understand these terms in any sense, that would justify the power in question, would give to Congress an unlimited power; would render nugatory the enumeration of particular powers; would supercede all the powers reserved to the state governments. These terms are copied from the articles of confederation; had it ever been pretended, that they were to be understood otherwise than as here explained?

It had been said that "general welfare" meant cases in which a general power might be exercised by Congress, without interfering with the powers of the States; and that the establishment of a National Bank was of this sort. There were, he said, several answers to this novel doctrine.

1. The proposed Bank would interfere so as indirectly to defeat a State Bank at the same place. 2. It would directly interfere with the rights of the States, to prohibit as well as to establish Banks, and the circulation of Bank Notes. He mentioned a law of Virginia, actually prohibiting the circulation

of notes payable to bearer. 3. Interference with the power of the States was no constitutional criterion of the power of Congress. If the power was not given, Congress could not exercise it; if given, they might exercise it, altho it should interfere with the laws, or even the constitution of the States. 4. If Congress could incorporate a Bank, merely because the act would leave the States free to establish Banks also; any other incorporations might be made by Congress. They could incorporate companies of manufacturers, or companies for cutting canals, or even religious societies, leaving similar incorporations by the States, like State Banks to themselves: Congress might even establish religious teachers in every parish, and pay them out of the Treasury of the United States, leaving other teachers unmolested in their functions. These inadmissible consequences condemned the controverted principle.

The case of the Bank established by the former Congress, had been cited as a precedent. This was known, he said, to have been the child of necessity. It never could be justified by the regular powers of the articles of confederation. Congress betrayed a consciousness of this in recommending to the States to incorporate the Bank also. They did not attempt to protect the Bank Notes by penalties against counterfeiters. These were reserved wholly to the authority of the States.

The second clause to be examined is that, which empowers Congress to borrow money.

Is this a bill to borrow money? It does not borrow a shilling. . . .

To say that the power to borrow involves a power of creating the ability, where there may be the will, to lend, is not only establishing a dangerous principle, as will be immediately shewn, but is as forced a construction, as to say that it involves the power of compelling the will, where there may be the ability, to lend.

The *third* clause is that which gives the power to pass all laws necessary and proper to execute the specified powers.

Whatever meaning this clause may have, none can be admitted, that would give an unlimited discretion to Congress.

Its meaning must, according to the natural and obvious force of the terms and the context, be limited to means *necessary* to the *end*, and *incident* to the *nature* of the specified powers. . . .

The essential characteristic of the government, as composed of limited and enumerated powers, would be destroyed: If instead of direct and incidental means, any means could be used, which in the language of the preamble to the bill, 'might be conceived to be conducive to the successful conducting of the finances; or might be conceived to tend to give facility to the obtaining of loans.' . . .

If, proceeded he, Congress, by virtue of the power to borrow, can create the means of lending, and in pursuance of these means, can incorporate a Bank, they may do any thing whatever creative of like means. . . .

If, again, Congress by virtue of the power to borrow money, can create the ability to lend, they may by virtue of the power to levy money, create the ability to pay it. The ability to pay taxes depends on the general wealth of the society, and this, on the general prosperity of agriculture, manufactures and commerce. Congress then may give bounties and make regulations on all of these objects.

The States have, it is allowed on all hands, a concurrent right to lay and collect taxes. This power is secured to them not by its being expressly reserved, but by its not being ceded by the constitution. The reasons for the bill cannot be admitted, because they would invalidate that right; why may it not be *conceived* by Congress, that an uniform and exclusive imposition of taxes, would not less than the proposed Banks 'be *conducive* to the successful conducting of the national finances, and *tend to give facility* to the obtaining of revenue, for the use of the government?'

The doctrine of implication is always a tender one. The danger of it has been felt in other governments. The delicacy was felt in the adoption of our own; the danger may also be felt, if we do not keep close to our chartered authorities.

Mark the reasoning on which the validity of the bill depends. To borrow money is made the end and the accumulation of capitals, *implied* as the *means*. The accumulation of capitals is then the end, and a bank implied as the means. The bank is then the end, and a charter of incorporation, a monopoly, capital punishments, *implied* as the *means*.

If implications, thus remote and thus multiplied, can be linked together, a chain may be formed that will reach every object of legislation, every object within the whole compass of political economy.

The latitude of interpretation required by the bill is condemned by the rule furnished by the constitution itself.

Congress have power "to regulate the value of money"; yet it is expressly added not left to be implied, that counterfeitors may be punished.

They have the power "to declare war," to which armies are more incident, than incorporated Banks, to borrowing; yet is expressly added, the power "to raise and support armies"; and to this again, the express power "to make rules and regulations for the government of armies"; a like remark is applicable to the powers as to a navy.

The regulation and calling out of the militia are more appurtenant to war, than the proposed bank, to borrowing; yet the former is not left to construction.

The very power to borrow money is a less remote implication from the power of war, than an incorporated monopoly bank, from the power of borrowing—yet the power to borrow is not left to implication.

It is not pretended that every insertion or omission in the constitution is the effect of systematic attention. This is not the character of any human work, particularly the work of a body of men. The examples cited, with others that might be added, sufficiently inculcate nevertheless a rule of interpretation, very different from that on which the bill rests. They condemn the exercise of any power, particularly a great and important power, which is not evidently and necessarily involved in an express power.

It cannot be denied that the power proposed to be exercised is an important power.

As a charter of incorporation the bill creates an artificial person previously not existing in law. It confers important civil rights and attributes, which could not otherwise be claimed. It is, though not precisely similar, at least equivalent, to the naturalization of an alien, by which certain new civil characters are acquired by him. Would Congress have had the power to naturalize, if it had not been expressly given?

In the power to make bye laws, the bill delegated a sort of legislative power, which is unquestionably an act of a high and important nature. He took notice of the only restraint on the bye laws, that they were not to be contrary to the law and the constitution of the bank; and asked what law was intended; if the law of the United States, the scantiness of their code would give a power, never before given to a corporation—and obnoxious to the States, whose laws would then be superceded not only by the laws of Congress, but by the bye laws of a corporation within their own jurisdiction. If the law intended, was the law of the State, then the State might make laws that would destroy an institution of the United States.

The bill gives a power to purchase and hold lands; Congress themselves could not purchase lands within a State "without the consent of its legislature." How could they delegate a power to others which they did not possess themselves?

It takes from our successors, who have equal rights with ourselves, and with the aid of experience will be more capable of deciding on the subject, an opportunity of exercising that right, for an immoderate term.

It takes from our constituents the opportunity of deliberating on the untried measure, although their hands are also to be tied by it for the same term.

It involves a monopoly, which affects the equal rights of every citizen.

It leads to a penal regulation, perhaps capital punishments, one of the most solemn acts of sovereign authority.

From this view of the power of incorporation exercised in the bill, it could never be deemed an accessary or subaltern power, to be deduced by implication, as a means of executing another power; it was in its nature a distinct, an independent and substantive prerogative, which not being enumerated in the constitution could never have been meant to be included in it, and not being included could never be rightfully exercised.

He here adverted to a distinction, which he said had not been sufficiently kept in view, between a power necessary and proper for the government or union, and a power necessary and proper for executing the enumerated powers. In the latter case, the powers included in each of the enumerated powers were not expressed, but to be drawn from the nature of each. In the former, the powers composing the government were expressly enumerated. This constituted the peculiar nature of the government, no power therefore not enumerated, could be inferred from the general nature of government. Had the power of making treaties, for example, been omitted, however necessary it might have been, the defect could only have been lamented, or supplied by an amendment of the constitution.

But the proposed bank could not even be called necessary to the government; at most it could be but convenient. Its uses to the government could be supplied by keeping the taxes a little in advance—by loans from individuals—by the other banks, over which the government would have equal command; nay greater, as it may grant or refuse to these the privilege, made a free and irrevocable gift to the proposed bank, of using their notes in the federal revenue.

He proceeded next to the contemporary expositions given to the constitution.

The defence against the charge founded on the want of a bill of rights, presupposed, he said, that the powers not given were retained; and that those given were not to be extended by remote implications. On any other supposition, the power of Congress to abridge the freedom of the press, or the rights of conscience, could not have been disproved.

The explanations in the state conventions all turned on the same fundamental principle, and on the principle that the terms necessary and proper gave no additional powers to those enumerated. . . .

In fine, if the power were in the constitution, the immediate exercise of it cannot be essential—if not there, the exercise of it involves the guilt of usurpation, and establishes a precedent of interpretation, levelling all the barriers which limit the powers of the general government, and protect those of the state governments. If the point be doubtful only, respect for ourselves, who ought to shun the appearance of precipitancy and ambition; respect for our successors, who ought not lightly to be deprived of the opportunity of exercising the rights of legislation; respect for our constituents who have had no opportunity of making known their sentiments, and who are themselves to be bound down to the measure for so long a period; all these considerations require that the irrevocable decision should at least be suspended until another session.

It appeared on the whole, he concluded, that the power exercised by the bill was condemned by the silence of the constitution; was condemned by the rule of interpretation arising out of the constitution; was condemned by its tendency to destroy the main characteristic of the constitution; was condemned by the expositions of the friends of the constitution, whilst depending before the public; was condemned by the apparent intention of the parties which ratified the constitution; was condemned by the explanatory amendments proposed by Congress themselves to the Constitution; and he hoped it would receive its final condemnation, by the vote of this house.

"Jefferson's Opinion on the Constitutionality of a National Bank" (1791)

The bill for establishing a National Bank undertakes among other things:

1. To form the subscribers into a corporation.

2. To enable them in their corporate capacities to receive grants of land; and so far is against the laws of *Mortmain*.

3. To make alien subscribers capable of holding lands, and so far is against the laws of *Alienage*.

4. To transmit these lands, on the death of a proprietor, to a certain line of successors; and so far changes the course of *Descents*.

5. To put the lands out of the reach of forfeiture or escheat, and so far is against the laws of *Forfeiture and Escheat*.

6. To transmit personal chattels to successors in a certain line and so far is against the laws of *Distribution*.

7. To give them the sole and exclusive right of banking under the national authority; and so far is against the laws of Monopoly.

8. To communicate to them a power to make laws paramount to the laws of the States; for so they must be construed, to protect the institution from the control of the State legislatures, and so, probably, they will be construed.

I consider the foundation of the Constitution as laid on this ground: That "all powers not delegated to the United States, by the Constitution, nor prohibited by it to the States, are reserved to the States or to the people." [XIIth amendment.] To take a single step beyond the boundaries thus specially drawn around the powers of Congress, is to take possession of a boundless field of power, no longer susceptible of any definition.

The incorporation of a bank, and the powers assumed by this bill, have not, in my opinion, been delegated to the United States, by the Constitution.

They are not among the powers specially enumerated: for these are:

1. A power to lay taxes for the purpose of paying the debts of the United States; but no debt is paid by this bill, nor any tax laid. Were it a bill to raise money, its origination in the Senate would condemn it by the Constitution.

2. "To borrow money." But this bill neither borrows money nor ensures the borrowing it. The proprietors of the bank will be just as free as any other money holders, to lend or not to lend their money to the public. The operation proposed in the bill first, to lend them two millions, and then to borrow them back again, cannot change the nature of the latter act, which will still be

a payment, and not a loan, call it by what name you please.

3. To "regulate commerce with foreign nations, and among the States, and with the Indian tribes." To erect a bank, and to regulate commerce, are very different acts. He who erects a bank, creates a subject of commerce in its bills, so does he who makes a bushel of wheat, or digs a dollar out of the mines; yet neither of these persons regulates commerce thereby. To make a thing which may be bought and sold, is not to prescribe regulations for buying and selling. Besides, if this was an exercise of the power of regulating commerce, it would be void, as extending as much to the internal commerce of every State, as to its external. For the power given to Congress by the Constitution does not extend to the internal regulation of the commerce of a State, (that is to say of the commerce between citizen and citizen,) which remain exclusively with its own legislature; but to its external commerce only, that is to say, its commerce with another State, or with foreign nations, or with the Indian tribes. Accordingly the bill does not propose the measure as a regulation of trade, but as "productive of considerable advantages to trade." Still less are these powers covered by any other of the special enumerations.

Nor are they within either of the general phrases, which are the two following:

1. To lay taxes to provide for the general welfare of the United States, that is to say, "to lay taxes for the purpose of providing for the general welfare." For the lay-

ing of taxes is the power, and the general welfare the purpose for which the power is to be exercised. They are not to lay taxes ad libitum for any purpose they please; but only to pay the debts or provide for the welfare of the Union. In like manner, they are not to do anything they please to provide for the general welfare, but only to lay taxes for that purpose. To consider the latter phrase, not as describing the purpose of the first, but as giving a distinct and independent power to do any act they please, which might be for the good of the Union, would render all the preceding and subsequent enumerations of power completely useless.

It would reduce the whole instrument to a single phrase, that of instituting a Congress with power to do whatever would be for the good of the United States; and, as they would be the sole judges of the good or evil, it would be also a power to do whatever evil they please.

It is an established rule of construction where a phrase will bear either of two meanings, to give it that which will allow some meaning to the other parts of the instrument, and not that which would render all the others useless. Certainly no such universal power was meant to be given them. It was intended to lace them up straitly within the enumerated powers, and those without which, as means, these powers could not be carried into effect. It is known that the very power now proposed *as a means* was rejected as *an end* by the Convention which formed the Constitution. A proposition was made to them to authorize Congress to open canals, and an amendatory one to empower them to incorporate. But the whole was rejected, and one of the reasons for rejection urged in debate was, that then they would have a power to erect a bank, which would render the great cities, where there were prejudices and jealousies on the subject, adverse to the reception of the Constitution.

2. The second general phrase is, "to make all laws *necessary* and proper for carrying into execution the enumerated powers." But they can all be carried into execution without a bank. A bank therefore is not *necessary*, and consequently not authorized by this phrase.

It has been urged that a bank will give great facility or convenience in the collection of taxes, Suppose this were true: yet the Constitution allows only the means which are "*necessary*," not those which are merely "convenient" for effecting the enumerated powers. If such a latitude of construction be allowed to this phrase as to give any non-enumerated power, it will go to everyone, for there is not one which ingenuity may not torture into a *convenience* in some instance *or other*, to *some one* of so long a list of enumerated powers. It would swallow up all the delegated powers, and reduce the whole to one power, as before observed. Therefore it was that the Constitution restrained them to the *necessary* means, that is to say, to those means without which the grant of power would be nugatory.

But let us examine this convenience and see what it is. The report on this subject states the only *general* convenience to be, the preventing the transportation and re-transportation of money between the States and the treasury, (for I pass over the increase of circulating medium, ascribed to it as a want, and which, according to my ideas of paper money, is clearly a demerit.) Every State will have to pay a sum of tax money into the treasury; and the treasury will have to pay, in every State, a part of the interest on the public debt, and salaries to the officers of government resident in that State. In most of the States there will still be a surplus of tax money to come up to the seat of government for the officers residing there. The payments of interest and salary in each State may be made by treasury orders on the State collector. This will take up the greater part of the money he has collected in his State, and consequently prevent the great mass of it from being drawn out of the State. If there be a balance of commerce in favor of that State against the one in which the government resides, the surplus of taxes will be remitted by the bills of exchange drawn for that commercial balance. And so it must be if there was a bank. But if there be no balance of commerce, either direct or circuitous, all the banks in the world could not bring up the surplus of taxes, but in the form of money. Treasury orders then, and bills of exchange may prevent the displacement of the main mass of the money collected, without the aid of any bank; and where these fail, it cannot be prevented even with that aid.

Perhaps, indeed, bank bills may be a more *convenient* vehicle than treasury orders. But a little *difference* in the degree of *convenience* cannot constitute the necessity which the Constitution makes the ground for assuming any non-enumerated power.

Besides, the existing banks will, without a doubt, enter into arrangements for lending their agency, and the more favorable, as there will be a competition among them for it; whereas the bill delivers us up bound to the national bank, who are free to refuse all arrangement, but on their own terms, and the public not free, on such refusal, to employ any other bank. That of Philadelphia I believe, now does this business, by their post-notes, which, by an arrangement with the treasury, are paid by any State collector to whom they are presented. This expedient alone suffices to prevent the existence of that *necessity* which may justify the assumption of a non-enumerated power as a means for carrying into effect an enumerated one. The thing may be done, and has been done, and well done, without this assumption, therefore it does not stand on that degree of *necessity* which can honestly justify it.

It may be said that a bank whose bills would have a currency all over the States, would be more convenient than one whose currency is limited to a single State. So it would be still more convenient that there should be a bank, whose bills should have a currency all over the world. But it does not follow from this superior conveniency, that there exists anywhere a power to establish such a bank; or that the world may not go on very well without it.

Can it be thought that the Constitution intended that for a shade or two of *convenience*, more or less, Congress should be authorized to break down the most ancient and fundamental laws of the several States; such as those against Mortmain, the laws of Alienage, the rules of descent, the acts of distribution, the laws of escheat and forfeiture, the laws of monopoly? Nothing but a necessity invincible by any other means, can justify such a prostitution of laws, which constitute the pillars of our whole system of jurisprudence. Will Congress be too strait-laced to carry the Constitution into honest effect, unless they may pass over the foundation-laws of the State government for the slightest convenience of theirs?

The negative of the President is the shield provided by the Constitution to protect against the invasions of the legislature: 1. The right of the Executive. 2. Of the Judiciary. 3. Of the States and State legislatures. The present is the case of a right remaining exclusively with the States, and consequently one of those intended by the Constitution to be placed under its protection.

It must be added, however, that unless the President's mind on a view of everything which is urged for and against this bill, is tolerably clear that it is unauthorized by the Constitution; if the pro and the con hang so even as to balance his judgment, a just respect for the wisdom of the legislature would naturally decide the balance in favor of their opinion. It is chiefly for cases where they are clearly misled by error, ambition, or interest, that the Constitution has placed a check in the negative of the President.

Though the Constitution controls the laws of Mortmain so far as to permit Congress itself to hold land for certain purposes, yet not so far as to permit them to communicate a similar right to other corporate bodies.

-T. J.

"Hamilton's Opinion as to the Constitutionality of a National Bank" (1791)

The Secretary of the Treasury having perused with attention the papers containing the opinions of the Secretary of State and Attorney General, concerning the constitutionality of the bill for establishing a National Bank, proceeds, according to the order of the President, to submit the reasons which have induced him to entertain a different opinion.

It will naturally have been anticipated, that in performing this task, he would feel uncommon solicitude. Personal considerations alone, arising from the reflection that the measure originated with him, would be sufficient to produce it. The sense which he has manifested of the great importance of such an institution to the successful administration of the department under his particular care, and an expectation of serious ill consequences to result from a failure of the measure, do not permit him to be without anxiety on public accounts. But the chief solicitude arises from a firm persuasion, that principles of construction like those espoused by the Secretary of State and the Attorney General, would be fatal to the just and indispensable authority of the United States.

In entering upon the argument, it ought to be premised, that the objections of the Secretary of State and Attorney General are founded on a general denial of the authority of the United States to erect corporations. The latter, indeed, expressly admits, that if there be any thing in the bill which is not warranted by the Constitution, it is the clause of incorporation.

Now it appears to the Secretary of the Treasury that this general principle is inherent in the very definition of government, and essential to every step of the progress to be made by that of the United States, namely: That every power vested in a government is in its nature sovereign, and includes, by force of the term, a right to employ all the means requisite, and fairly applicable to the attainment of the ends of such power; and which are not precluded by restrictions and exceptions specified in the Constitution, or not immoral, or not contrary to the essential ends of political society.

This principle, in its application to government in general, would be admitted as an axiom; and it will be incumbent upon those who may incline to deny it, to prove a distinction, and to show that a rule which, in the general system of things, is essential to the preservation of the social order, is inapplicable to the United States.

The circumstance that the powers of sovereignty are in this country divided between the National and State governments, does not afford the distinction required. It does not follow from this, that each of the portions of powers delegated to the one or to the other, is not sovereign with regard to its proper objects. It will only follow from it, that each has sovereign power as to certain things, and not as to other things. To deny that the government of the United States has sovereign power as to its declared purposes and trusts, because its power does not extend to all cases would be equally to deny that the State governments have sovereign power in any case, because their power does not extend to every case. The tenth section of the first article of the constitution exhibits a long list of very important things which they may not do. And thus the United States would furnish the singular spectacle of a political society without sovereignty, or of a people governed, without government.

If it would be necessary to bring proof to a proposition so clear, as that which affirms that the powers of the federal government, as to its objects, were sovereign, there is a clause of its Constitution which would be decisive. It is that which declares, that the Constitution, and the laws of the United States, made in pursuance of it, and all treaties made, or which shall be made, under their authority, shall be the supreme law of the land. The power which can create the supreme law of the land in any case, is doubtless sovereign as to such case.

This general and indisputable principle puts at once an end to the abstract question, whether the United States have power to erect a corporation; that is to say, to give a legal or artificial capacity to one or more persons, distinct from the natural. For it is unquestionably incident to sovereign power to erect corporations, and consequently to that of the United States, in relation to the objects intrusted to the management of the government. The difference is this: where the authority of the government is general, it can create corporations in all cases, where it is confined to certain branches of legislation, it can create corporations only in those cases.

Here then, as far as concerns the reasonings of the Secretary of State and the Attorney General, the affirmative of the constitutionality of the bill might be permitted to rest. It will occur to the President, that the principle here advanced has been untouched by either of them.

For a more complete elucidation of the point, nevertheless, the arguments which they have used against the power of the government to erect corporations, however foreign they are to the great and fundamental rule which has been stated, shall be particularly examined. . . .

The first of these arguments is, that the foundation of the Constitution is laid on this ground "That all powers not delegated to the United States by the Constitution, nor prohibited to it by the States, are reserved for the States, or to the people." Whence it is meant to be inferred, that Congress can in no case exercise any power not included in those not enumerated in the Constitution. And it is affirmed, that the power of erecting a corporation is not included in any of the enumerated powers.

The main proposition here laid down, in its true signification is not to be questioned. It is nothing more than a consequence of this republican maxim, that all government is a delegation of power. But how much is delegated in each case, is a question of fact, to be made out by fair reasoning and construction, upon the particular provisions of the Constitution, taking as guides the general principles and general ends of government.

It is not denied that there are implied as well as express powers, and that the former are as effectually delegated as the latter. . . .

. . . It is conceded that implied powers are to be considered as delegated equally with express ones. Then it follows, that as a power of erecting a corporation may as well be implied as any other thing, it may as well be employed as an instrument or mean of carrying into execution any of the specified powers, as any other instrument or mean whatever. The only question must be in this, as in every other case, whether the mean to be employed or in this instance, the corporation to be erected, has a natural relation to any of the acknowledged objects or lawful ends of the government. Thus a corporation may not be erected by Congress for superintending the police of the city of Philadelphia, because they are not authorized to regulate the police of that city. But one may be erected in relation to the collection of the taxes, or to the trade with foreign countries, or to the trade between the States, or with the Indian Tribes; because it is the province of the federal government to regulate those objects. . . .

A strange fallacy seems to have crept into the manner of thinking and reasoning upon the subject. Imagination appears to have been unusually busy concerning it. An incorporation seems to have been regarded as some great, independent substantive thing; as a political end of peculiar magnitude and moment; whereas it is truly to be considered as a quality, capacity, or mean to an end. . . .

To this mode of reasoning respecting the right of employing all the means requisite to the execution of the specified powers of the government, it is objected, that none but necessary and proper means are to be employed; and the Secretary of State maintains, that no means are to be considered as necessary but those without which the grant of the power would be nugatory. Nay, so far does he go in his restrictive interpretation of the word, as even to make the case of necessity which shall warrant the constitutional exercise of the power to depend on casual and temporary circumstances; an idea which alone refutes the construction. The expediency of exercising a particular power, at a particular time, must, indeed depend on circumstances, but the constitutional right of exercising it must be uniform and invariable, the same to-day, as to-morrow. . . .

It is essential to the being of the national government, that so erroneous a conception of the meaning of the word necessary should be exploded.

It is certain that neither the grammatical nor popular sense of the term requires that construction. According to both, necessary often means no more than needful, requisite, incidental, useful, or conducive to. . . . And it is the true one in which it is to be understood as used in the Constitution. The whole turn of the clause containing it indicates, that it was the intent of the Convention, by that clause, to give a liberal latitude to the exercise of the specified powers. The expressions have peculiar comprehensiveness. They are thought "to make all laws necessary and proper for carrying into execution the foregoing powers, and all other powers vested by the Constitution in the government of the United States, or in any department or officer thereof."

To understand the word as the Secretary of State does, would be to depart from its obvious and popular sense, and to give it a restrictive operation, an idea never before entertained. It would be to give it the same force as if the word absolutely or indispensably had been prefixed to it.

Such a construction would beget endless uncertainty and embarrassment. The cases must be palpable and extreme, in which it could be pronounced, with certainty, that a measure was absolutely necessary, or one, without which, the exercise of a given power would be nugatory. There are few measures of any government which would stand so severe a test. To insist upon it, would be to make the criterion of the exercise of any implied power, a case of extreme necessity; which is rather a rule to justify the overleaping of the bounds of constitutional authority, than to govern the ordinary exercise of it.

It may be truly said of every government, as well as of that of the United States, that it has only a right to pass such laws as are necessary and proper to accomplish the objects intrusted to it. For no government has a right to do merely what it pleases. Hence, by a process of reasoning similar to that of the Secretary of State, it might be proved that neither of the State governments has a right to incorporate a bank. It might be shown that all the public business of the state, could be performed without a bank, and inferring thence that it was unnecessary. . . . It is to be remembered that there is no express power in any State constitution to erect corporations.

The degree in which a measure is necessary, can never be a test of the legal right to adopt it; that must be a matter of opinion, and can only be a test of expediency. The relation between the measure and the end; between the nature of the mean employed toward the execution of a power, and the object of that power must be the criterion of constitutionality, not the more or less of necessity or utility.

The practice of the government is against the rule of construction advocated by the Secretary of State. Of this, the Act concerning lighthouses, beacons, buoys, and public piers, is a decisive example. This, doubtless, must be referred to the power of regulating trade, and is fairly relative to it. But it cannot be affirmed that the exercise of that power in this instance was strictly necessity or that the power itself would be nugatory, without that of regulating establishments of this nature.

This restrictive interpretation of the word necessary is also contrary to this sound maxim of construction, namely, that the powers contained in a constitution of government, especially those which concern the general administration of the affairs of a country, its finances, trade, defense, etc., ought to be construed liberally in advancement of the public good. This rule does not depend on the particular form of a government, or on the particular demarcation of the boundaries of its powers, but on the nature and objects of government itself. The means by which national exigencies are to be provided for, national inconveniencies obviated, national prosperity promoted, are of such infinite variety, extent, and complexity, that there must of necessity be great latitude of discretion in the selection and application of those means. Hence, consequently, the necessity and propriety of exercising the authorities intrusted to a government on principles of liberal construction.

The Attorney General admits the rule, but takes a distinction between a State and the Federal Constitution. The latter, he thinks, ought to be construed with greater strictness, because there is more danger of error in defining partial than General powers. But the reason of the rule forbids such a distinction. This reason is, the variety and extent of public exigencies, a far greater proportion of which, and of a far more critical kind, are objects of National than of State administration. The greater danger of error, as far as it is supposable, may be a prudential reason for caution in practice, but it cannot be a rule of restrictive interpretation. . . .

The truth is, that difficulties on this point are inherent in the nature of the Federal Constitution; they result inevitably from a division of the legislative power. The consequence of this division is, that there will be cases clearly within the power of the national government; others, clearly without its powers; and a third class, which will leave room for controversy and difference of opinion, and concerning which a reasonable latitude of judgment must be allowed.

But the doctrine which is contended for is not chargeable with the consequence imputed to it. It does not affirm that the national government is sovereign in all respects, but that it is sovereign to a certain extent; that is, to the extent of the objects of its specified powers.

It leaves therefore a criterion of what is constitutional, and of what is not so. This criterion is the end, to which the measure relates as a mean. If the end be clearly comprehended within any of the specified powers, and if the measure have an obvious relation to that end, and is not forbidden by any particular provision of the Constitution, it may safely be deemed to come within the compass of the national authority. There is also this further criterion, which may materially assist the decision: Does the proposed measure abridge a pre-existing right of any State or of any individual? If it does not, there is a strong presumption in favor of its constitutionality. . . .

The general objections, which are to be inferred from the reasonings of the Secretary of State and of the Attorney General, to the doctrine which has been advanced, have been stated, and it is hoped satisfactorily answered. Those of a more particular nature shall now be examined.

The Secretary of State introduces his opinion with an observation, that the proposed incorporation undertakes to create certain capacities, properties, or attributes, which are against the laws of alienage, descents, escheat and forfeiture, distribution and monopoly, and to confer a power to make laws paramount to those of the States. And nothing, says he, in another place, but necessity, invincible by other means, can justify such a prostration of laws, which constitute the pillars of our whole system of jurisprudence, and are the foundation laws of the State governments. . . .

But if it were even to be admitted that the erection of a corporation is a direct alteration of the state laws, in the enumerated particulars; it would do nothing toward proving that the measure was unconstitutional. If the government of the United States can do no act which amounts to an alteration of a State law, all its powers are nugatory; for almost every new law is an alteration, in some way or other, of an old law, either common or statute. . . .

There are two points in the suggestions of the Secretary

of State, which have been noted, that are peculiarly incorrect. One is, that the proposed incorporation is against the laws of monopoly, because it stipulates an exclusive right of banking under the national authority; the other, that it gives power to the institution to make laws paramount to those of the States.

But, with regard to the first: The bill neither prohibits any State from erecting as many banks as they please, nor any number of individuals from associating to carry on the business, and consequently, is free from the charge of establishing a monopoly. . . .

And with regard to the second point, there is still less foundation. The by-laws of such an institution as a bank can operate only on its own members can only concern the disposition of its own property, and must essentially resemble the rules of a private mercantile partnership. They are expressly not to be contrary to law; and law must here mean the law of a State, as well as of the United States. There never can be a doubt, that a law of a corporation, if contrary to a law of a State, must be overruled as void unless the law of the State is contrary to that of the United States and then the question will not be between the law of the State and that of the corporation, but between the law of the State and that of the United States. . . .

Most of the arguments of the Secretary of State, which have not been considered in the foregoing remarks, are of a nature rather to apply to the expediency than to the constitutionality of the bill. . . .

The proposed bank is to consist of an association of persons for the purpose of creating a joint capital, to be employed chiefly and essentially in loans. So far the object is not only lawful, but it is the mere exercise of a right which the law allows to every individual. The Bank of New York, which is not incorporated, is an example of such an association. The bill proposes in addition, that the government shall become a joint proprietor in this undertaking, and that it shall permit the bills of the company, payable on demand, to be receivable in its revenues; and stipulates that it shall not grant privileges, similar to those which are to be allowed to this company, to any others. All this is incontrovertibly within the compass of the discretion of the government. The only question is, whether it has a right to incorporate this company, in order to enable it the more effectually to accomplish ends which are in themselves lawful.

To establish such a right, it remains to show the relation of such an institution to one or more of the specified powers of the government. Accordingly it is affirmed that it has a relation, more or less direct, to the power of collecting taxes, to that of borrowing money, to that of regulating trade between the States, and to those of raising and maintaining fleets and armies. To the two former the relation may be said to be immediate; and in the last place it will be argued, that it is clearly within the provision which authorizes the making of all needful rules and regulations concerning the property of the United States, as the same has been practiced upon by the government.

A bank relates to the collection of taxes in two ways indirectly, by increasing the quantity of circulating medium and quickening circulation, which facilitates the means of paying directly, by creating a convenient species of medium in which they are to be paid.

To designate or appoint the money or thing in which taxes are to be paid, is not only a proper, but a necessary exercise of the power of collecting them. . . .

A bank has a direct relation to the power of borrowing money, because it is an usual, and in sudden emergencies an essential, instrument in the obtaining of loans to government.

A nation is threatened with a war, large sums are wanted on a sudden to make the requisite preparations. Taxes are laid for the purpose, but it requires time to obtain the benefit of them. Anticipation is indispensable. If there be a bank the supply can at once be had. If there be none, loans from individuals must be sought. The progress of these is often too slow for the exigency: in some situations they are not practicable at all. Frequently when they are, it is of great consequence to be able to anticipate the product of them by advances from a bank. . . .

The institution of a bank has also a natural relation to the regulation of trade between the States, in so far as it is conducive to the creation of a convenient medium of exchange between them, and to the keeping up a full circulation, by preventing the frequent displacement of the metals in reciprocal remittances. Money is the very hinge on which commerce turns. And this does not mean merely gold and silver; many other things have served the purpose, with different degrees of utility. Paper has been extensively employed. . . .

A hope is entertained that it has, by this time, been made to appear, to the satisfaction of the President, that a bank has a natural relation to the power of collecting taxes—to that of regulating trade—to that of providing for the common defense and that, as the bill under consideration contemplates the government in the light of a joint proprietor of the stock of the bank, it brings the case within the provision of the clause of the Constitution which immediately respects the property of the United States.

Under a conviction that such a relation subsists, the Secretary of the Treasury, with all deference, conceives that it will result as a necessary consequence from the position that all the specified powers of the government are sovereign, as to the proper objects that the incorporation of a bank is a constitutional measure, and that the objections taken to the bill, in this respect, are ill-founded. . . .

PHILADELPHIA FEBRUARY 23D. 1791.

HAMILTON V. JAMES MADISON

(*War Powers*)

The Proclamation of Neutrality of 1793, by George Washington

Whereas it appears that a state of war exists between Austria, Prussia, Sardinia, Great-Britain, and the United Netherlands, of the one part, and France on the other; and the duty and interest of the United States require, that they should with sincerity and good faith adopt and pursue a conduct friendly and impartial toward the belligerent powers:

I have therefore thought fit by these presents to declare the disposition of the United States to observe the conduct aforesaid towards those Powers respectfully; and to exhort and warn the citizens of the United States carefully to avoid all acts and proceedings whatsoever, which may in any manner tend to contravene such disposition.

And I do hereby also make known, that whatsoever of the citizens of the United States shall render himself liable to punishment or forfeiture under the law of nations, by committing, aiding or abetting hostilities against any of the said powers, or by carrying to any of them those articles, which are deemed contraband by the *modern* usage of nations, will not receive the protection of the United States, against such punishment or forfeiture: and further, that I have given instructions to those officers, to whom it belongs, to cause prosecutions to be instituted against all persons, who shall, within the cognizance of the courts of the United States, violate the Law of Nations, with respect to the powers at war, or any of them.

In testimony whereof, I have caused the Seal of the United States of America to be affixed to these presents, and signed the same with my hand. Done at the city of Philadelphia, the twenty-second day of April, one thousand seven hundred and ninety-three, and of the Independence of the United States of America the seventeenth.

GEORGE WASHINGTON
APRIL 22, 1793

THE PACIFICUS-HELVIDIUS DEBATE

Pacificus No. 1, by Alexander Hamilton (1793)

. . . The objections which have been raised against the Proclamation of Neutrality lately issued by the President have been urged in a spirit of acrimony and invective, which demonstrates, that more was in view than merely a free discussion of an important public measure; that the discussion covers a design of weakening the confidence of the People in the author of the measure; in order to remove or lessen a powerful obstacle to the success of an opposition to the Government, which however it may change its form, according to circumstances, seems still to be adhered to and pursued with persevering Industry. . . .

The objections in question fall under [four] heads—

1. That the Proclamation was without authority

2. That it was contrary to our treaties with France

3. That it was contrary to the gratitude, which is due from this to that country; for the succours rendered us in our own Revolution.

4. That it was out of time & unnecessary. . . .

The inquiry then is—what department of the Government of the UStates is the prop(er) one to make a declaration of Neutrality in the cases in which the engagements (of) the Nation permit and its interests require such a declaration.

A correct and well informed mind will discern at once that it can belong neit(her) to the Legislative nor Judicial Department and of course must belong to the Executive.

The Legislative Department is not the *organ* of intercourse between the UStates and foreign Nations. It is charged neither with *making* nor *interpreting* Treaties. It is therefore not naturally that Organ of the Government which is to pronounce the existing condition of the Nation, with regard to foreign Powers, or to admonish the Citizens of their obligations and duties as founded upon that condition of things. Still less is it charged with enforcing the execution and observance of these obligations and those duties.

It is equally obvious that the act in question is foreign to the Judiciary Department of the Government. The province of that Department is to decide litigations in particular cases. It is indeed charged with the interpretation of treaties; but it exercises this function only in the litigated cases; that is where contending parties bring before it a specific controversy. It has no concern with pronouncing upon the external political relations of Treaties between Government and Government. This position is too plain to need being insisted upon.

It must then of necessity belong to the Executive Department to exercise the function in Question—when a proper case for the exercise of it occurs.

It appears to be connected with that department in various capacities, as the *organ* of intercourse between the Nation and foreign Nations—as the interpreter of the National Treaties in those cases in which the Judiciary is not competent, that is in the cases between Government and Government—

as that Power, which is charged with the Execution of the Laws, of which Treaties form a part—as that Power which is charged with the command and application of the Public Force. . . .

The second Article of the Constitution . . . establishes this general Proposition, That "The Executive Power shall be vested in a President of the United States of America." . . .

The general doctrine then of our constitution is, that the Executive Power of the Nation is vested in the President; subject only to the *exceptions* and *qu[a]lifications* which are expressed in the instrument.

Two of these have been already noticed—the participation of the Senate in the appointment of Officers and the making of Treaties. A third remains to be mentioned the right of the Legislature "to declare war and grant letters of marque and reprisal." . . .

If the Legislature have a right to make war on the one hand—it is on the other the duty of the Executive to preserve Peace till war is declared; and in fulfilling that duty, it must necessarily possess a right of judging what is the nature of the obligations which the treaties of the Country impose on the Government; and when in pursuance of this right it has concluded that there is nothing in them inconsistent with a *state* of neutrality, it becomes both its province and its duty to enforce the laws incident to that state of the Nation. The Executive is charged with the execution of all laws, the laws of Nations as well as the Municipal law, which recognises and adopts those laws. It is consequently bound, by faithfully executing the laws of neutrality, when that is the state of the Nation, to avoid giving a cause of war to foreign Powers. . . .

The right of the Executive to receive ambassadors and other public Ministers may serve to illustrate the relative duties of the Executive and Legislative Departments. This right includes that of judging, in the case of a Revolution of Government in a foreign Country, whether the new rulers are competent organs of the National Will and ought to (be) recognised or not: And where a treaty antecedently exists between the UStates and such nation that right involves the power of giving operation or not to such treaty. For until the new Government is *acknowleged*, the treaties between the nations, as far at least as regards *public* rights, are of course suspended.

This power of determ[in]ing virtually in the case supposed upon the operation of national Treaties as a consequence, of the power to receive ambassadors and other public Ministers, is an important instance of the right of the Executive to decide the obligations of the Nation with regard to foreign Nations. To apply it to the case of France, if the(re) had been a Treaty of alliance *offensive* (and) defensive between the UStates and that Coun(try), the unqualified acknowlegement of the new Government would have put the UStates in a condition to become an associate in the War in which France was engaged—and would have laid the Legislature under an obligation, if required, and there was otherwise no valid excuse, of exercising its power of declaring war.

This serves as an example of the right of the Executive, in certain cases, to determine the condition of the Nation, though it may consequentially affect the proper or improper exercise of the Power of the Legislature to declare war. The Executive indeed cannot control the exercise of that power—further than by the exer[c]ise of its general right of objecting to all acts of the Legislature; liable to being overruled by two thirds of both houses of Congress. The Legislature is free to perform its own duties according to its own sense of them—though the Executive in the exercise of its constitutional powers, may establish an antecedent state of things which ought to weigh in the legislative decisions. From the division of the Executive Power there results, in referrence to it, a *concurrent* authority, in the distributed cases.

Hence in the case stated, though treaties can only be made by the President and Senate, their activity may be continued or suspended by the President alone. . . .

It deserves to be remarked, that as the participation of the senate in the making of Treaties and the power of the Legislature to declare war are exceptions out of the general "Executive Power" vested in the President, they are to be construed strictly—and ought to be extended no further than is essential to their execution.

While therefore the Legislature can alone declare war, can alone actually transfer the nation from a state of Peace to a state of War—it belongs to the "Executive Power," to do whatever else the laws of Nations cooperating with the Treaties of the Country enjoin, in the intercourse of the UStates with foreign Powers.

In this distribution of powers the wisdom of our constitution is manifested. It is the province and duty of the Executive to preserve to the Nation the blessings of peace. The Legislature alone can interrupt those blessings, by placing the Nation in a state of War.

Helvidius No. 1,
by James Madison (1793)

. . . Let us examine.

In the general distribution of powers, we find that of declaring war expressly vested in the Congress, where every other legislative power is declared to be vested, and without any other qualification than what is common to every other legislative act. The constitutional idea of this power would seem then clearly to be, that it is of a legislative and not an executive nature.

This conclusion becomes irresistible, when it is recollected, that the constitution cannot be supposed to have placed either any power legislative in its nature, entirely among executive powers, or any power executive in its nature, entirely among legislative powers, without charging the constitution, with that kind of intermixture and consolidation of different powers, which would violate a fundamental principle in the organization of free governments. If it were not unnecessary to enlarge on this topic here, it could be shewn, that the constitution was originally vindicated, and has been constantly expounded, with a disavowal of any such intermixture.

The power of treaties is vested jointly in the President and in the Senate, which is a branch of the legislature. From this arrangement merely, there can be no inference that would necessarily exclude the power from the executive class: since the senate is joined with the President in another power, that of appointing to offices, which as far as relate to executive offices at least, is considered as of an executive nature. Yet on the other hand, there are sufficient indications that the power of treaties is regarded by the constitution as materially different from mere executive power, and as having more affinity to the legislative than to the executive character. . . .

. . . [T]hat treaties when formed according to the constitutional mode, are confessedly to have the force and operation of *laws*, and are to be a rule for the courts in controversies between man and man, as much as any *other laws*. They are even emphatically declared by the constitution to be "the supreme law of the land."

So far the argument from the constitution is precisely in opposition to the doctrine. As little will be gained in its favour from a comparison of the two powers, with those particularly vested in the President alone.

As there are but few it will be most satisfactory to review them one by one.

"The President shall be commander in chief of the army and navy of the United States, and of the militia when called into the actual service of the United States."

There can be no relation worth examining between this power and the general power of making treaties. And instead of being analogous to the power of declaring war, it affords a striking illustration of the incompatibility of the two powers in the same hands. Those who are to *conduct a war* cannot in the nature of things, be proper or safe judges, whether *a war ought* to be *commenced*, *continued*, or *concluded*. They are barred from the latter functions by a great principle in free government, analogous to that which separates the sword from the purse, or the power of executing from the power of enacting laws. . . .

Thus it appears that by whatever standard we try this doctrine, it must be condemned as no less vicious in theory than it would be dangerous in practice. It is countenanced neither by the writers on law; nor by the nature of the powers themselves; nor by any general arrangements or particular expressions, or plausible analogies, to be found in the constitution.

Whence then can the writer have borrowed it?

There is but one answer to this question.

The power of making treaties and the power of declaring war, are *royal prerogatives* in the *British government*, and are accordingly treated as Executive prerogatives by *British commentators*. . . .

HELVIDIUS.

Helvidius No. 2,
by James Madison (1793)

. . . Leaving however to the leisure of the reader deductions which the author having omitted might not chuse to own, I proceed to the examination of one, with which that liberty cannot be taken.

"However true it may be (says he) that the right of the legislature to declare war *includes the right of judging* whether the legislature be under obligations to make war or not, it will not follow that the executive is *in any case* excluded from a *similar right* of judging in the execution of its own functions." . . .

A concurrent authority in two independent departments to perform the same function with respect to the same thing, would be as awkward in practice, as it is unnatural in theory.

If the legislature and executive have both a right to judge of the obligations to make war or not, it must sometimes happen, though not at present, that they will judge differently. The executive may proceed to consider the question to-day, may determine that the United States are not bound to take part in a war, and in the execution of its functions proclaim that determination to all the world. To-morrow, the legislature may follow in the consideration of the same subject, may determine that the obligations impose war on the United States, and *in the execution of its functions*, enter into a *constitutional declaration*, expressly contradicting the *constitutional procla-mation*.

In what light does this present the constitution to the people who established it? In what light would it present to the world, a nation, thus speaking, thro' two different organs, equally constitutional and authentic, two opposite languages, on the same subject and under the same existing circumstances?

But it is not with the legislative rights alone that this doc-trine interferes. The rights of the judiciary may be equally invaded. For it is clear that if a right declared by the constitu-tion to be legislative, and actually vested by it in the legislature, leaves, notwithstanding, a similar right in the executive when-ever a case for exercising it occurs, *in the course of its functions*: a right declared to be judiciary and vested in that department may, on the same principle, be assumed and exercised by the executive *in the course of its functions*: and it is evident that oc-casions and pretexts for the latter interference may be as fre-quent as for the former. So again the judiciary department may find equal occasions in the execution of *its* functions, for usurping the authorities of the executive: and the legislature for stepping into the jurisdiction of both. And thus all the powers of government, of which a partition is so carefully made among the several branches, would be thrown into ab-solute hotchpot, and exposed to a general scramble. . . .

HELVIDIUS.

Part IV

PERSONALITY OR POLITICS?

☆

Alexander Hamilton's Insults

Just as Hamilton had fallen out with his former ally James Madison, he would also find himself at odds with the second president, John Adams. The two had helped to found the Federalist Party, united in their belief that the national government needed strong powers to preserve liberty. But during the Adams administration, Hamilton became convinced that President Adams was not the right person to wield his office's power. This debate is personal, with Hamilton aiming squarely at the specific actions of Adams. But as you read, reflect on whether Hamilton's criticism reveals any new trepidation about the power of presidents—worries he earlier dismissed during the ratification debate and the Washington administration. A flawed president cannot help but raise questions about the nature of an office, imbued—as Hamilton intended for it to be—with great power.

The second conflict we examine in this section would lead to Hamilton's death. In a letter to Hamilton, Burr argued that he had been informed his longtime rival's insults went beyond mere political disagreement and had disparaged him personally. Hamilton protested in his response that the accusations were unfounded. This is not so much a philosophical debate as a personal fight with the threat of a pistol duel—a somewhat common way for former military officers to resolve disputes— simmering in the background. The documents demonstrate to contemporary readers how violence sometimes lurked beneath the surface of political debate in the early republic. The back and forth did not end well and resulted in Burr's request for a duel. Hamilton's final piece of writing, excerpted here, sees him struggling to explain why he would attend the duel despite common objections to the practice of resolving personal disputes with violence. Burr's pistol would put an abrupt end to the life and writings of Hamilton, one of our most important framers and thinkers about liberty.

"Special Session Message to Congress (XYZ Affair)," by John Adams (1797)

Gentlemen of the Senate and Gentlemen of the House of Representatives:

The personal inconveniences to the members of the Senate and of the House of Representatives in leaving their families and private affairs at this season of the year are so obvious that I the more regret the extraordinary occasion which has rendered the convention of Congress indispensable.

It would have afforded me the highest satisfaction to have been able to congratulate you on a restoration of peace to the nations of Europe whose animosities have endangered our tranquillity; but we have still abundant cause of gratitude to the Supreme Dispenser of National Blessings for general health and promising seasons, for domestic and social happiness, for the rapid progress and ample acquisitions of industry through extensive territories, for civil, political, and religious liberty. While other states are desolated with foreign war or convulsed with intestine divisions, the United States present the pleasing prospect of a nation governed by mild and equal laws, generally satisfied with the possession of their rights, neither envying the advantages nor fearing the power of other nations, solicitous only for the maintenance of order and justice and the preservation of liberty, increasing daily in their attachment to a system of government in proportion to their experience of its utility, yielding a ready and general obedience to laws flowing from the reason and resting on the only solid foundation—the affections of the people.

It is with extreme regret that I shall be obliged to turn your thoughts to other circumstances, which admonish us that some of these felicities may not be lasting. But if the tide of our prosperity is full and a reflux commencing, a vigilant circumspection becomes us, that we may meet our reverses with fortitude and extricate ourselves from their consequences with all the skill we possess and all the efforts in our power.

In giving to Congress information of the state of the Union and recommending to their consideration such measures as appear to me to be necessary or expedient, according to my constitutional duty, the causes and the objects of the present extraordinary session will be explained.

After the President of the United States received information that the French Government had expressed serious discontents at some proceedings of the Government of these States said to affect the interests of France, he thought it expedient to send to that country a new minister, fully instructed to enter on such amicable discussions and to give such candid explanations as might happily remove the discontents and suspicions of the French Government and vindicate the conduct of the United States. For this purpose he selected from among his fellow-citizens a character whose integrity, talents, experience, and services had placed him in the rank of the most esteemed and respected in the nation.

The direct object of his mission was expressed in his letter of credence to the French Republic, being "to maintain that good understanding which from the commencement of the alliance had subsisted between the two nations, and to efface unfavorable impressions, banish suspicions, and restore that cordiality which was at once the evidence and pledge of a friendly union." And his instructions were to the same effect, "faithfully to represent the disposition of the Government and people of the United States (their disposition being one), to remove jealousies and obviate complaints by shewing that they were groundless, to restore that mutual confidence which had been so unfortunately and injuriously impaired, and to explain the relative interests of both countries and the real sentiments of his own."

A minister thus specially commissioned it was expected would have proved the instrument of restoring mutual confidence between the two Republics. The first step of the French Government corresponded with that expectation. A few days before his arrival at Paris the French minister of foreign relations informed the American minister then resident at Paris of the formalities to be observed by himself in taking leave, and by his successor preparatory to his reception. These formalities they observed, and on the 9th of December presented officially to the minister of foreign relations, the one a copy of his letters of recall, the other a copy of his letters of credence.

These were laid before the Executive Directory. Two days afterwards the minister of foreign relations informed the recalled American minister that the Executive Directory had determined not to receive another minister plenipotentiary from the United States until after the redress of grievances demanded of the American Government, and which the French Republic had a right to expect from it.

The American minister immediately endeavored to ascertain whether by refusing to receive him it was intended that he should retire from the territories of the French Republic, and verbal answers were given that such was the intention of the Directory. For his own justification he desired a written answer, but obtained none until toward the last of January, when, receiving notice in writing to quit the territories of the Republic, he proceeded to Amsterdam, where he proposed to wait for instruction from this government.

During his residence at Paris cards of hospitality were refused him, and he was threatened with being subjected to the jurisdiction of the minister of police; but with becoming firmness he insisted on the protection of the law of nations due to him as the known minister of a foreign power.

You will derive further information from his dispatches, which will be laid before you.

As it is often necessary that nations should treat for the mutual advantage of their affairs, and especially to accommodate and terminate differences, and as they can treat only by ministers, the right of embassy is well known and established by the law and usage of nations. The refusal on the part of France to receive our minister is, then, the denial of a right; but the refusal to receive him until we have acceded to their demands without discussion and without investigation is to treat us neither as allies nor as friends, nor as a sovereign state.

With this conduct of the French government it will be proper to take into view the public audience given to the late minister of the United States on his taking leave of the Executive Directory. The speech of the President discloses sentiments more alarming than the refusal of a minister, because more dangerous to our independence and union, and at the same time studiously marked with indignities toward the government of the United States.

It evinces a disposition to separate the people of the United States from the government, to persuade them that they have different affections, principles, and interests from those of their fellow citizens whom they themselves have chosen to manage their common concerns, and thus to produce divisions fatal to our peace. Such attempts ought to be repelled with a decision which shall convince France and the world that we are not a degraded people, humiliated under a colonial spirit of fear and sense of inferiority, fitted to be the miserable instruments of foreign influence, and regardless of national honor, character, and interest.

I should have been happy to have thrown a veil over these transactions if it had been possible to conceal them; but they have passed on the great theater of the world, in the face of all Europe and America, and with such circumstances of publicity and solemnity that they can not be disguised and will not soon be forgotten. They have inflicted a wound in the American breast. It is my sincere desire, however, that it may be healed.

It is my sincere desire, and in this I presume I concur with you and with our constituents, to preserve peace and friendship with all nations; and believing that neither the honor nor the interest of the United States absolutely forbid the repetition of advances for securing these desirable objects with France, I shall institute a fresh attempt at negotiation, and shall not fail to promote and accelerate an accommodation on terms compatible with the rights, duties, interests, and honor of the nation. If we have committed errors, and these can be demonstrated, we shall be willing to correct them; if we have done injuries, we shall be willing on conviction to redress them; and equal measures of justice we have a right to expect from France and every other nation.

The diplomatic intercourse between the United States and France being at present suspended, the Government has no means of obtaining official information from that country.

Nevertheless, there is reason to believe that the Executive Directory passed a decree on the 2nd of March last contravening in part the treaty of amity and commerce of 1778, injurious to our lawful commerce and endangering the lives of our citizens. A copy of this decree will be laid before you.

While we are endeavoring to adjust all our differences with France by amicable negotiation, the progress of the war in Europe, the depredations on our commerce, the personal injuries to our citizens, and the general complexion of affairs render it my indispensable duty to recommend to your consideration effectual measures of defense.

The commerce of the United States has become an interesting object of attention, whether we consider it in relation to the wealth and finances or the strength and resources of the nation. With a seacoast of near 2,000 miles in extent, opening a wide field for fisheries, navigation, and commerce, a great portion of our citizens naturally apply their industry and enterprise to these objects. Any serious and permanent injury to commerce would not fail to produce the most embarrassing disorders. To prevent it from being undermined and destroyed it is essential that it receive an adequate protection.

The naval establishment must occur to every man who considers the injuries committed on our commerce, the insults offered to our citizens, and the description of vessels by which these abuses have been practiced. As the sufferings of our mercantile and seafaring citizens can not be ascribed to the omission of duties demandable, considering the neutral situation of our country, they are to be attributed to the hope of impunity arising from a supposed inability on our part to afford protection. To resist the consequences of such impressions on the minds of foreign nations and to guard against the degradation and servility which they must finally stamp on the American character is an important duty of Government.

A naval power, next to the militia, is the natural defense of the United States. The experience of the last war would be sufficient to shew that a moderate naval force, such as would be easily within the present abilities of the Union, would have been sufficient to have baffled many formidable transportations of troops from one State to another, which were then practiced. Our seacoasts, from their great extent, are more easily annoyed and more easily defended by a naval force than any other. With all the materials our country abounds; in skill our naval architects and navigators are equal to any, and commanders and seamen will not be wanting.

But although the establishment of a permanent system of naval defense appears to be requisite, I am sensible it can not be formed so speedily and extensively as the present crisis demands. Hitherto I have thought proper to prevent the sailing of armed vessels except on voyages to the East Indies, where general usage and the danger from pirates appeared to render the permission proper. Yet the restriction has originated solely from a wish to prevent collisions with the powers at war, contravening the act of Congress of June, 1794, and not from any doubt entertained by me of the policy and propriety of permitting our vessels to employ means of defense while engaged in a lawful foreign commerce.

It remains for Congress to prescribe such regulations as will enable our seafaring citizens to defend themselves against violations of the law of nations, and at the same time restrain them from committing acts of hostility against the powers at war. In addition to this voluntary provision for defense by individual citizens, it appears to me necessary to equip the frigates, and provide other vessels of inferior force, to take under convoy such merchant vessels as shall remain unarmed.

The greater part of the cruisers whose depredations have been most injurious have been built and some of them partially equipped in the United States. Although an effectual remedy may be attended with difficulty, yet I have thought it my duty to present the subject generally to your consideration. If a mode can be devised by the wisdom of Congress to prevent the resources of the United States from being converted into the means of annoying our trade, a great evil will be prevented. With the same view, I think it proper to mention that some of our citizens resident abroad have fitted out privateers, and others have voluntarily taken the command, or entered on board of them, and committed spoliations on the commerce of the United States. Such unnatural and iniquitous practices can be restrained only by severe punishments.

But besides a protection of our commerce on the seas, I think it highly necessary to protect it at home, where it is collected in our most important ports. The distance of the United States from Europe and the well-known promptitude, ardor, and courage of the people in defense of their country happily diminish the probability of invasion. Nevertheless, to guard against sudden and predatory incursions the situation of some of our principal seaports demands your consideration. And as our country is vulnerable in other interests besides those of its commerce, you will seriously deliberate whether the means of general defense ought not to be increased by an addition to the regular artillery and cavalry, and by arrangements for forming a provisional army.

With the same view, and as a measure which, even in a time of universal peace; ought not to be neglected, I recommend to your consideration a revision of the laws for organizing, arming, and disciplining the militia, to render that natural and safe defense of the country efficacious.

Although it is very true that we ought not to involve our-selves in the political system of Europe, but to keep ourselves always distinct and separate from it if we can, yet to effect this separation, early, punctual, and continual information of the current chain of events and of the political projects in contemplation is no less necessary than if we were directly concerned in them. It is necessary, in order to the discovery of the efforts made to draw us into the vortex, in season to make preparations against them.

However we may consider ourselves, the maritime and commercial powers of the world will consider the United States of America as forming a weight in that balance of power in Europe which never can be forgotten or neglected. It would not only be against our interest, but it would be doing wrong to one-half of Europe, at least, if we should voluntarily throw ourselves into either scale.

It is a natural policy for a nation that studies to be neutral to consult with other nations engaged in the same studies and pursuits. At the same time that measures might be pursued with this view, our treaties with Prussia and Sweden, one of which is expired and the other near expiring, might be renewed.

Gentlemen of the House of Representatives:

It is particularly your province to consider the state of the public finances, and to adopt such measures respecting them as exigencies shall be found to require. The preservation of public credit, the regular extinguishment of the public debt, and a provision of funds to defray any extraordinary expenses will of course call for your serious attention. Although the imposition of new burthens can not be in itself agreeable, yet there is no ground to doubt that the American people will ex-pect from you such measures as their actual engagements, their present security, and future interests demand.

Gentlemen of the Senate and Gentlemen of the House of Representatives:

The present situation of our country imposes an obligation on all the departments of government to adopt an explicit and decided conduct. In my situation an exposition of the principles by which my administration will be governed ought not to be omitted.

It is impossible to conceal from ourselves or the world what has been before observed, that endeavors have been employed to foster and establish a division between the government and people of the United States. To investigate the causes which have encouraged this attempt is not necessary; but to repel, by decided and united councils, insinuations so derogatory to the honor and aggressions so dangerous to the Constitution, union, and even independence of the nation is an indispensable duty.

It must not be permitted to be doubted whether the people of the United States will support the government established by their voluntary consent and appointed by their free choice, or whether, by surrendering themselves to the direction of foreign and domestic factions, in opposition to their own government, they will forfeit the honorable station they have hitherto maintained.

For myself, having never been indifferent to what concerned the interests of my country, devoted the best part of my life to obtain and support its independence, and constantly witnessed the patriotism, fidelity, and perseverance of my fellow citizens on the most trying occasions, it is not for me to hesitate or abandon a cause in which my heart has been so long engaged.

Convinced that the conduct of the government has been just and impartial to foreign nations, that those internal regulations which have been established by law for the preservation of peace are in their nature proper, and that they have been fairly executed, nothing will ever be done by me to impair the national engagements, to innovate upon principles which have been so deliberately and uprightly established, or to surrender in any manner the rights of the government. To enable me to maintain this declaration I rely, under God, with entire confidence on the firm and enlightened support of the national legislature and upon the virtue and patriotism of my fellow citizens.

JOHN ADAMS.

"Concerning the Public Conduct and Character of John Adams, Esq.," by Alexander Hamilton (1800)

Sir,

Some of the warm personal friends of Mr. Adams are taking unwearied pains to disparage the motives of those Federalists, who advocate the equal support of Gen. Pinckney, at the approaching election of President and Vice-President. They are exhibited under a variety of aspects equally derogatory. Sometimes they are versatile, factious spirits, who cannot be long satisfied with any chief, however meritorious:—Sometimes they are ambitious spirits, who can be contented with no man that will not submit to be governed by them:—Sometimes they are intriguing partisans of Great-Britain, who, devoted to the advancement of her views, are incensed against Mr. Adams for the independent impartiality of his conduct. . . .

It is necessary, for the public cause, to repel these slanders; by stating the real views of the persons who are calumniated, and the reasons of their conduct.

In executing this task, with particular reference to myself, I ought to premise, that the ground upon which I stand, is different from that of most of those who are confounded with me as in pursuit of the same plan. While our object is common, our motives are variously dissimilar. A part, well affected to Mr. Adams, have no other wish than to take a double chance against Mr. Jefferson. Another part, feeling a diminution of confidence in him, still hope that the general tenor of his conduct will be essentially right. Few go as far in their objections as I do. Not denying to Mr. Adams patriotism and integrity, and even talents of a certain kind, I should be deficient in candor, were I to conceal the conviction, that he does not possess the talents adapted to the *Administration* of Government, and that there are great and intrinsic defects in his character, which unfit him for the office of Chief Magistrate.

To give a correct idea of the circumstances which have gradually produced this conviction, it may be useful to retrospect to an early period.

I was one of that numerous class who had conceived a high veneration for Mr. Adams, on account of the part he acted in the first stages of our revolution. My imagination had exalted him to a high eminence, as a man of patriotic, bold, profound, and comprehensive mind. But in the progress of the war, opinions were ascribed to him, which brought into question, with me, the solidity of his understanding. He was represented to be of the number of those who favored the enlistment of our troops annually, or for short periods, rather than for the term of the war; a blind and infatuated policy, directly contrary to the urgent recommendation of General Washington, and which had nearly proved the ruin of our cause. He was also said to have advocated the project of appointing yearly a new Commander of the Army; a project which, in any service, is likely to be attended with more evils than benefits; but which, in ours, at the period in question, was chimerical, from the want of persons qualified to succeed, and pernicious, from the peculiar fitness of the officer first appointed, to strengthen, by personal influence, the too feeble cords which bound to the service, an ill-paid, ill-clothed, and undisciplined soldiery.

It is impossible for me to assert, at this distant day, that these suggestions were brought home to Mr. Adams in such a manner as to ascertain their genuineness; but I distinctly remember their existence, and my conclusion from them; which was, that, if true, they proved this gentleman to be infected with some visionary notions, and that he was far less able in the practice, than in the theory, of politics. I remember also, that they had the effect of inducing me to qualify the admiration which I had once entertained for him. . . .

In this disposition I was, when just before the close of the war, I became a member of Congress.

The situation in which I found myself there, was far from being inauspicious to a favorable estimate of Mr. Adams.

Upon my first going into Congress, I discovered symptoms of a party already formed, too well disposed to subject the interests of the United States to the management of France. Though I felt, in common with those who had participated in our Revolution, a lively sentiment of good will towards a power, whose co-operation, however it was and ought to have been dictated by its own interest, had been extremely useful to us, and had been afforded in a liberal and handsome manner; yet, tenacious of the real independence of our country, and dreading the preponderance of foreign influence, as the natural disease of popular government, I was struck with disgust at the appearance, in the very cradle of our Republic, of a party actuated by an undue complaisance to foreign power; and I resolved at once to resist this bias in our affairs: a resolution, which has been the chief cause of the persecution I have endured in the subsequent stages of my political life. . . .

. . . I . . . adopted an opinion, which all my subsequent experience has confirmed, that he is a man of an imagination sublimated and eccentric; propitious neither to the regular display of sound judgment, nor to steady perseverance in a systematic plan of conduct; and I began to perceive what has been since too manifest, that to this defect are added the unfortunate foibles of a vanity without bounds, and a jealousy capable of discoloring every object. . . .

This opinion, however, which I have avowed, did not prevent my entering cordially into the plan of supporting Mr. Adams for the office of Vice-President, under the new Constitution. I still thought that he had high claims upon the public gratitude, and possessed a substantial worth of character, which might atone for some great defects. In addition to this, it was well known, that he was a favorite of New-England, and it was obvious that his union with General Washington would tend to give the government, in its outset, all the strength which it could derive from the character of the two principal magistrates.

But it was deemed an essential point of caution to take care, that accident or an intrigue of the opposers of the Government, should not raise Mr. Adams, instead of General Washington, to the first place. This, every friend of the Government would have considered as a disastrous event; as well because it would have displayed a capricious operation of the system in elevating to the first station, a man intended for the second; as because it was conceived that the incomparably superior weight and transcendant popularity of Gen. Washington, rendered his presence at the head of the Government, in its first organization, a matter of primary and indispensable importance. It was therefore agreed that a few votes should be diverted from Mr. Adams to other persons, so as to insure to General Washington a plurality.

Great was my astonishment, and equally great my regret, when, afterwards, I learned from persons of unquestionable veracity, that Mr. Adams had complained of unfair treatment, in not having been permitted to take an equal chance with General Washington, by leaving the votes to an uninfluenced current.

The extreme egotism of the temper, which could blind a man to considerations so obvious as those that had recommended the course pursued, cannot be enforced by my comment. It exceeded all that I had imagined, and shewed, in too strong a light, that the vanity which I have ascribed to him, existed to a degree that rendered it more than a harmless foible. . . .

The epoch at length arrived, when the retreat of General Washington made it necessary to fix upon a successor. By this time, men of principal influence in the Federal Party, whose situation had led them to an intimate acquaintance with Mr. Adams's character, began to entertain serious doubts about his fitness for the station; yet, his pretensions, in several respects, were so strong, that after mature reflection, they thought it better to indulge their hopes than to listen to their fears. To this conclusion, the desire of preserving harmony in the Federal Party, was a weighty inducement. Accordingly it was determined to support Mr. Adams for the Chief Magistracy.

It was evidently of much consequence to endeavor to have an eminent Federalist Vice-President. Mr. Thomas Pinckney, of South Carolina, was selected for this purpose. This gentleman, too little known in the North, had been all his life time distinguished in the South, for the mildness and amiableness of his manners, the rectitude and purity of his morals, and the soundness and correctness of his understanding, accompanied by a habitual discretion and self-command, which has often occasioned a parallel to be drawn between him and the venerated Washington. . . .

Well-informed men knew that the event of the Election was extremely problematical; and, while the friends of Mr. Jefferson predicted his success with sanguine confidence, his opposers feared that he might have at least an equal chance with any Federal Candidate.

To exclude him, was deemed, by the Federalists, a primary object. Those of them who possessed the best means of judging, were of opinion that it was far less important, whether Mr. Adams or Mr. Pinckney was the successful Candidate, than that Mr. Jefferson should not be the person; and on this principle, it was understood among them, that the two first mentioned gentlemen should be equally supported; leaving to casual accessions of votes in favor of the one or the other, to turn the scale between them.

In this plan I united with good faith; in the resolution, to which I scrupulously adhered, of giving to each Candidate an equal support. This was done, wherever my influence extended; as was more particularly manifested in the State of New-York, where all the Electors were my warm personal or political friends, and all gave a concurrent vote for the two Federal Candidates.

It is true that a faithful execution of this plan would have given Mr. Pinckney a somewhat better chance than Mr. Adams; nor shall it be concealed, that an issue favorable to the former would not have been disagreeable to me; as indeed I declared at the time, in the circles of my confidential friends. My position was, that if chance should decide in favor of Mr. Pinckney, it probably would not be a misfortune; since he, to every essential qualification for the office, added a temper far more discreet and conciliatory than that of Mr. Adams. . . .

. . . The considerations which had reconciled me to the success of Mr. Pinckney, were of a nature exclusively public. They resulted from the disgusting egotism, the distempered jealousy, and the ungovernable indiscretion of Mr. Adams's temper, joined to some doubts of the correctness of his maxims of Administration. Though in matters of Finance he had acted with the Federal Party; yet he had, more than once, broached theories at variance with his practice. And in conversation, he repeatedly made excursions in the field of foreign politics, which alarmed the friends of the prevailing system.

The plan of giving equal support to the two Federalist Candidates, was not pursued. Personal attachment for Mr. Adams, especially in the New-England States, caused a number of the votes to be withheld from Mr. Pinckney, and thrown away. The result was, that Mr. Adams was elected President by a majority of two votes, and Mr. Jefferson Vice-President.

This issue demonstrated the wisdom of the plan which had been abandoned, and how greatly, in departing from it, the cause had been sacrificed to the man. But for a sort of miracle, the departure would have made Mr. Jefferson President. . . .

No one, sincere in the opinion that this gentleman was an ineligible and dangerous Candidate, can hesitate in pronouncing, that in dropping Mr. Pinckney, too much was put at hazard; and that those who promoted the other course, acted with prudence and propriety.

It is a fact, which ought not to be forgotten, that Mr. Adams, who had evinced discontent, because he had not been permitted to take an equal chance with General Washington, was enraged with all those who had thought that Mr. Pinckney ought to have had an equal chance with him. But in this there is perfect consistency. The same turn of temper is the solution of the displeasure in both cases.

It is to this circumstance of the equal support of Mr. Pinckney, that we are in a great measure to refer the serious scism which has since grown up in the Federal Party.

Mr. Adams never could forgive the men who had been engaged in the plan; though it embraced some of his most partial admirers. He has discovered bitter animosity against several of them. Against me, his rage has been so vehement, as to have caused him more than once, to forget the decorum, which, in his situation, ought to have been an inviolable law. It will not appear an exaggeration to those who have studied his character, to suppose that he is capable of being alienated from a system to which he has been attached, because it is upheld by men whom he hates. How large a share this may have had in some recent aberrations, cannot easily be determined.

Occurrences which have either happened or come to light since the election of Mr. Adams to the Presidency, confirming my unfavorable forebodings of his character, have given new and decisive energy, in my mind, to the sentiment of his unfitness for the station. . . .

It is in regard to our foreign relations, that the public measures of Mr. Adams first attract criticism.

It will be recollected that General Pinckney . . . the gentleman now supported together with Mr. Adams, had been deputed by President Washington, as successor to Mr. Monroe, and had been refused to be received by the French Government in his quality of Minister Plenipotentiary.

This, among those of the well-informed, who felt a just sensibility for the honor of their country, excited much disgust and resentment. But the Opposition-Party, ever too ready to justify the French Government at the expense of their own, vindicated or apologized for the ill treatment: and the mass of the community, though displeased with it, did not appear to feel the full force of the indignity.

As a final effort for accommodation, and as a mean, in case of failure, of enlightening and combining public opinion, it was resolved to make another, and a more solemn, experiment, in the form of a commission of three.

This measure . . . was approved by all parties; by the Anti-federalists, because they thought no evil so great as the rupture with France; by the Federalists, because it was their system to avoid war with every power, if it could be done without the sacrifice of essential interests or absolute humiliation. . . .

The expediency of the step was suggested to Mr. Adams, through a Federal channel, a considerable time before he determined to take it. He hesitated whether it could be done after the rejection of General Pinckney, without national debasement. The doubt was an honorable one; it was afterwards very properly surrendered to the cogent reasons which pleaded for a further experiment.

The event of this experiment is fresh in our recollection. Our Envoys, like our Minister, were rejected. Tribute was demanded as a preliminary to negociation. To their immortal honor, though France at the time was proudly triumphant, they repelled the disgraceful pretension. Americans will never forget that General Pinckney was a member, and an efficient member, of this Commission.

This conduct of the French Government, in which it is difficult to say, whether despotic insolence or unblushing corruption was most prominent, electrified the American people with a becoming indignation. In vain the partisans of France attempted to extenuate. The public voice was distinct and audible. The nation, disdaining so foul an overture, was ready to encounter the worst consequences of resistance.

Without imitating the flatterers of Mr. Adams, who, in derogation from the intrinsic force of circumstances, and from the magnanimity of the nation, ascribe to him the whole merits of producing the spirit which appeared in the community, it shall with cheerfulness be acknowledged, that he took upon the occasion a manly and courageous lead—that he did all in his power to rouse the pride of the nation—to inspire it with a just sense of the injuries and outrages which it had experienced, and to dispose it to a firm and magnanimous resistance; and that his efforts contributed materially to the end.

The friends of the Government were not agreed as to ulterior measures. Some were for immediate and unqualified war; others for a more mitigated course; the dissolution of treaties, preparation of force by land and sea, partial hostilities of a defensive tendency; leaving to France the option of seeking accommodation, or proceeding to open war. The latter course prevailed. . . .

The latter conduct of the President forms a painful contrast to his commencement. Its effects have been directly the reverse. It has sunk the tone of the public mind—it has impaired the confidence of the friends of the Government in the Executive Chief—it has distracted public opinion—it has unnerved the public councils—it has sown the seeds of discord at home, and lowered the reputation of the Government abroad. . . .

Mr. Adams arrived at Philadelphia from his seat at Quincy. . . .

It was suggested to him, that it might be expedient to insert in his Speech of Congress, a sentiment of this import:

That after the repeatedly rejected advances of this country, its dignity required that it should be left with France in future to make the first overture; that if, desirous of reconciliation, she should evince the disposition by sending a Minister to this Government, he would be received with the respect due to his character, and treated with in the frankness of a sincere desire of accommodation.

The suggestion was received in a manner both indignant and intemperate.

Mr. Adams declared as a sentiment which he had adopted on mature reflection: *That if France should send a Minister to-morrow, he would order him back the day after.*

So imprudent an idea was easily refuted. Little argument was requisite to shew that by a similar system of retaliation, when one Government in a particular instance had refused the Envoy of another, nations might entail upon each other perpetual hostility; mutually barring the avenues of explanation.

In less than forty-eight hours from this extraordinary sally, the mind of Mr. Adams underwent a total revolution—he resolved not only to insert in his speech the sentiment which had been proposed to him, but to go farther, and to declare, that if France would give explicit assurances of receiving a Minister from this country, with due respect, he would send one.

In vain was this extension of the sentiment opposed by all his Ministers, as being equally incompatible with good policy, and with the dignity of the nation—he obstinately persisted, and the pernicious declaration was introduced.

I call it pernicious, because it was the ground-work of the false steps which have succeeded.

The declaration recommended to the President was a prudent one.

The measures of Congress, by their mitigated form, shewed that an eye had been still kept upon pacification. A numerous party were averse from war with France at any rate. In the rest of the community, a strong preference of honorable accommodation to final rupture was discernible, even amidst the effusions of resentment.

The charges which we had exhibited in the face of the world against the French Government, were of a high and disgraceful complexion; they had been urged with much point and emphasis.

To give an opening to France, to make conciliatory propositions, some salve for her pride was necessary. It was also necessary she should be assured that she would not expose herself to an affront by a refusal to receive the agent whom she might employ for that purpose. The declaration proposed fulfilled both objects.

It was likely to have another important advantage. It would be a new proof to the American people of the moderate and pacific temper of their Government; which would tend to preserve their confidence, and to dispose them more and more to meet inevitable extremities with fortitude and without murmurs.

But the supplement to the declaration was a blameable excess. It was more than sufficient for the ends to be answered. It waved the point of honor, which, after two rejections of our Ministers, required that the next Mission between the two countries, should proceed from France. After the mortifying humiliations we had endured, the national dignity demanded that this point should not be departed from without necessity. No such necessity could be pretended to exist: moreover, another mission by us would naturally be regarded as evidence of a disposition on our part to purchase the friendship of revolutionary France, even at the expense of honor;

an impression which could hardly fail to injure our interests with other countries: and the measure would involve the further inconvenience of transferring the negociation from this country, where our government could regulate it according to its own view of exigencies, to France, where that advantage would be enjoyed by her Government, and where the power of judging for us must be delegated to Commissioners; who, acting under immense individual responsibility, at a distance too great for consultation, would be apt to act with hesitancy and irresolution, whether the policy of the case required concession or firmness. This was to place it too much in the power of France to manage the progress of the negociation according to events. . . .

When the President pledged himself in his speech to send a minister, if satisfactory assurances of a proper reception were given, he must have been understood to mean such as were direct and official, not such as were both informal and destitute of a competent sanction.

Yet upon this loose and vague foundation, Mr. Adams precipitately nominated Mr. Murray as Envoy to the French Republic, without previous consultation with any of his Ministers. The nomination itself was to each of them, even to the Secretary of State, his Constitutional Counsellor, in similar affairs, the first notice of the project.

Thus was the measure wrong, both as to mode and substance.

A President is not bound to conform to the advice of his Ministers. He is even under no positive injunction to ask or require it. But the Constitution presumes that he will consult them; and the genius of our government and the public good recommend the practice. . . .

Very different from the practice of Mr. Adams was that

of the modest and sage Washington. He consulted much, pondered much, resolved slowly, resolved surely.

And as surely, Mr. Adams might have benefited by the advice of his ministers.

The stately system of not consulting Ministers is likely to have a further disadvantage. It will tend to exclude from places of primary trust, the men most fit to occupy them. . . .

Every thing that tends to banish from the Administration able men, tends to diminish the chances of able counsels. The probable operation of a system of this kind, must be to consign places of the highest trust to incapable honest men, whose inducement will be a livelihood, or to capable dishonest men, who will seek indirect indemnifications for the deficiency of direct and fair inducements.

The precipitate nomination of Mr. Murray, brought Mr. Adams into an aukward predicament.

He found it necessary to change his plan in its progress, and instead of one, to nominate three Envoys, and to superadd a promise, that, though appointed, they should not leave the United States till further and more perfect assurances were given by the French Government.

This remodification of the measure was a virtual acknowledgment that it had been premature. How unseemly was this fluctuation in the Executive Chief. It argued either instability of views, or want of sufficient consideration beforehand. The one or the other, in an affair of so great moment, is a serious reproach.

Additional and more competent assurances were received; but before the Envoys departed, intelligence arrived of a new Revolution in the French Government; which, in violation of the Constitution, had expelled two of the Directory.

Another Revolution: Another Constitution overthrown:

Surely here was reason for a pause, at least till it was ascertained that the new Directory would adhere to the engagement of its predecessors, and would not send back our Envoys with disgrace. . . .

Yet our Envoys were dispatched without a ratification of the assurance by the new Directory, at the hazard of the interests and the honor of the country.

Again, the dangerous and degrading system of not consulting Ministers, was acted upon. . . .

. . . Mr. Adams had the option of a substitute far preferable to the expedient which he chose.

He might secretly and confidentially have nominated one or more of our Ministers actually abroad for the purpose of treating with France; with *eventual* instructions predicated upon appearances of an approaching peace.

An expedient of this sort, merely provisionary, could have had none of the bad effects of the other. If the secret was kept, it could have had no inconvenient consequences; if divulged, it would have been deemed here and elsewhere, a prudent precaution only, recommended by the distant situation of the country, to meet future casualties, with which we might otherwise not have been able to keep pace. To the enemies of France, it could have given no ill impression of us; to France, no motive to forbear other conciliatory means, for one and the same reason, namely, because the operation was to be eventual. . . .

I have now gone through the principal circumstances in Mr. Adams's conduct, which have served to produce my disapprobation of him as Chief Magistrate. I pledge my veracity and honor, that I have stated none which are not either derived from my own knowledge, or from sources of information, in the highest degree, worthy of credit. . . .

Letter to Aaron Burr Denying the Accusations, by Alexander Hamilton (1804)

Sir:

I have maturely reflected on the subject of your letter of the 18th instant, and the more I have reflected, the more I have become convinced that I could not without manifest impropriety make the avowal or disavowal which you seem to think necessary.

The clause pointed out by Mr. Van Ness is in these terms: "I could detail to you a *still more despicable opinion* which General Hamilton has expressed of Mr. Burr." To endeavor to discover the meaning of this declaration, I was obliged to seek in the antecedent part of the letter for the opinion to which it referred, as having been already disclosed. I found it in these words: "General Hamilton and Judge Kent have declared *in substance* that they looked upon Mr. Burr to be *a dangerous man*, and one who *ought not to be trusted with the reins of Government*." The language of Dr. Cooper plainly implies that he considered this opinion of you, which he attributes to me, as a *despicable* one; but he affirms that I have expressed some other *still more despicable*; without, however mentioning to whom, when or where. 'Tis evident that the phrase "still more despicable" admits of infinite shades from very light to very dark. How am I to judge of the degree intended? Or how should I annex any precise idea to language so indefinite?

Between Gentlemen *despicable* and *more despicable* are not worth the pains of a distinction. When, therefore, you do not interrogate me as to the opinion which is specifically ascribed to me, I must conclude that you view it as within the limits to which the animadversions of political opponents, upon each other, may justifiably extend; and consequently as not warranting the idea of it which Dr. Cooper appears to entertain. If so, what precise inference could you draw as a guide for your future conduct, were I to acknowledge that I had expressed an opinion of you, *still more despicable*, than the one which is particularized? How could you be sure that even this opinion had exceeded the bounds which you would yourself deem admissible between political opponents?

But I forbear further comment on the embarrassment to which the requisition you have made naturally leads. The occasion forbids a more ample illustration, though nothing would be more easy than to pursue it.

Repeating that I cannot reconcile it with propriety to make the acknowledgement or denial you desire, I will add that I deem it inadmissible on principle, to consent to be interrogated as to the justness of the *inferences* which may be drawn by *others*, from whatever I may have said of a political opponent in the course of a fifteen years competition. If there were no other objection to it, this is sufficient, that it would tend to expose my sincerity and delicacy to injurious imputations from every person who may at any time have conceived that import of my expressions differently from what I may then have intended, or may afterwards recollect.

I stand ready to avow or disavow promptly and explicitly any precise or definite opinion which I may be charged with having declared to any Gentleman. More than this cannot fitly be expected from me; and especially it cannot reasonably be expected that I shall enter into an explanation upon a basis so vague as that which you have adopted. I trust upon more reflection you will see the matter in the same light with me. If not, I can only regret the circumstances and must abide the consequences.

The publication of Dr. Cooper was never seen by me 'till after the receipt of your letter.

I have the honor to be Sir Your obed. servt.

A. HAMILTON.

Letter to Alexander Hamilton on Alleged Personal Insults, by Aaron Burr (1804)

Sir

Mr. V Ness has this evening reported to me Verbally that you refuse to answer my last letter, that you consider the course I have taken as intemperate and unnecessary and some other conversation which it is improper that I should notice.

My request to you was in the first instance proposed in a form the most simple in order that you might give to the affair that course to which you might be induced by your temper and your knowledge of facts. I relied with unsuspecting faith that from the frankness of a Soldier and the Candor of a gentleman I might expect an ingenuous declaration; that if, as I had reason to believe, you had used expressions derogatory to my honor, you would have had the Spirit to Maintain or the Magnanimity to retract them, and, that if from your language injurious inferences had been improperly drawn, Sincerity and delicacy would have pointed out to you the propriety of correcting errors which might thus have been widely diffused.

With these impressions, I was greatly disappointed in receiving from you a letter which I could only consider as evasive and which in manner, is not altogether decorus. In one expectation however, I was not wholly deceived, for at the close of your letter I find an intimation, that if I should dislike your refusal to acknowledge or deny the charge, you were ready to meet the consequences. This I deemed a sort of defiance, and I should have been justified if I had chosen to make it the basis of an immediate message: Yet, as you had also said something (though in my opinion unfounded) of the indefiniteness of my request; as I believed that your communication was the offspring, rather of false pride than of reflection, and, as I felt the utmost reluctance to proceed to extremities while any other hope remained, my request was repeated in terms more definite. To this you refuse all reply, reposing, as I am bound to presume on the tender of an alternative insinuated in your letter.

Thus, Sir, you have invited the course I am about to pursue, and now by your silence impose it upon me. If therefore your determinations are final, of which I am not permitted to doubt, Mr. Van Ness is authorised to communicate my further expectations either to yourself or to such friend as you may be pleased to indicate.

I have the honor to be Your Ob st

A. BURR

On Dueling, by Alexander Hamilton (1804)

On my expected interview with Col Burr, I think it proper to make some remarks explanatory of my conduct, motives and views.

I am certainly desirous of avoiding this interview, for the most cogent reasons.

1. My religious and moral principles are strongly opposed to the practice of Duelling, and it would even give me pain to be obliged to shed the blood of a fellow creature in a private combat forbidden by the laws.

2. My wife and Children are extremely dear to me, and my life is of the utmost importance to them, in various views.

3. I feel a sense of obligation towards my creditors; who in case of accident to me, by the forced sale of my property, may be in some degree sufferers. I did not think my self at liberty, as a man of probity, lightly to expose them to this hazard.

4. I am conscious of no *ill-will* to Col Burr, distinct from political opposition, which, as I trust, has proceeded from pure and upright motives.

Lastly, I shall hazard much, and can possibly gain nothing by the issue of the interview.

But it was, as I conceive, impossible for me to avoid it. There were *intrinsick* difficulties in the thing, and *artificial* embarrassments, from the manner of proceeding on the part of Col Burr.

Intrinsick—because it is not to be denied, that my animadversions on the political principles character and views of Col Burr have been extremely severe, and on different occasions, I, in common with many others, have made very unfavourable criticisms on particular instances of the private conduct of this Gentleman.

In proportion as these impressions were entertained with sincerity and uttered with motives and for purposes, which might appear to me commendable, would be the difficulty (until they could be removed by evidence of their being erroneous), of explanation or apology. The disavowal required of me by Col Burr, in a general and indefinite form, was out of my power, if it had really been proper for me to submit to be so questionned; but I was sincerely of opinion, that this could not be, and in this opinion, I was confirmed by that of a very moderate and judicious friend whom I consulted. Besides that Col Burr appeared to me to assume, in the first instance, a tone unnecessarily peremptory and menacing, and in the second, positively offensive. Yet I wished, as far as might be practicable, to leave a door open to accommodation. This, I think, will be inferred from the written communications made by me and by my direction, and would be confirmed by the conversations between Mr van Ness and myself, which arose out of the subject.

I am not sure, whether under all the circumstances I did not go further in the attempt to accommodate, than a pun[c]tilious delicacy will justify. If so, I hope the motives I have stated will excuse me.

It is not my design, by what I have said to affix any odium on the conduct of Col Burr, in this case. He doubtless has heared of animadversions of mine which bore very hard upon him; and it is probable that as usual they were accompanied with some falshoods. He may have supposed himself under a necessity of acting as he has done. I hope the grounds of his proceeding have been such as ought to satisfy his own conscience.

I trust, at the same time, that the world will do me the Justice to believe, that I have not censured him on light grounds, or from unworthy inducements. I certainly have had strong reasons for what I may have said, though it is possible that in some particulars, I may have been influenced by misconstruction or misinformation. It is also my ardent wish that I may have been more mistaken than I think I have been, and that he by his future conduct may shew himself worthy of all confidence and esteem, and prove an ornament and blessing to his Country.

As well because it is possible that I may have injured Col Burr, however convinced myself that my opinions and declarations have been well founded, as from my general principles and temper in relation to similar affairs—I have resolved, if our interview is conducted in the usual manner, and it pleases God to give me the opportunity, to *reserve* and *throw away* my first fire, and I *have thoughts* even of *reserving* my second fire—and thus giving a double opportunity to Col Burr to pause and to reflect.

It is not however my intention to enter into any explanations on the ground. Apology, from principle I hope, rather than Pride, is out of the question.

To those, who with me abhorring the practice of Duelling

may think that I ought on no account to have added to the number of bad examples—I answer that my *relative* situation, as well in public as private aspects, enforcing all the considerations which constitute what men of the world denominate honor, impressed on me (as I thought) a peculiar necessity not to decline the call. The ability to be in future useful, whether in resisting mischief or effecting good, in those crises of our public affairs, which seem likely to happen, would probably be inseparable from a conformity with public prejudice in this particular.

Acknowledgments

I would like to thank all of the people who have helped bring this series to life by reading drafts, providing edits, and helping to put together the final versions. Aidan Calvelli provided careful editing and thoughtful input on all aspects of the series. Priyanka Podugu brought a keen eye to helping me compile materials, highlighting selections that brought out the key themes of liberty. My wife, Allison Brettschneider, was, as she always is, an invaluable partner in this work, giving substantive editorial feedback. David McNamee, Kevin McGravey, Megan Bird, Olivia Siemens, Amistad Meeks, Noah Klein, Rakhi Kundra, and Chris Woods all graciously read drafts and provided valuable comments and suggestions. I would also like to thank Elda Rotor and Elizabeth Vogt from Penguin for all they have done to make this series possible, and Rafe Sagalyn, my agent, for his continued support, encouragement, and guidance.

Unabridged Source Materials

PART I

Samuel Seabury. *Free Thoughts, On the Proceedings of the Continental Congress, Held at Philadelphia, Sept. 5, 1774* [. . .]. New York: James Rivington, 1774; Ann Arbor: Text Creation Partnership. http://name.umdl.umich.edu/N10731.0001.001.

Alexander Hamilton. A Full Vindication of the Measures of the Congress, from the Calumnies of Their Enemies [...]. New York: James Rivington, 1774; Founders Online, National Archive. https://founders.archives.gov/documents/ Hamilton/01-01-02-0054.

Alexander Hamilton, *The Farmer Refuted* [...]. New York, James Rivington, 1775; *Founders Online*, National Archives. https:// founders.archives.gov/documents/Hamilton/01-01-02-0057.

PART II

Brutus. "Essay I." October 1787. In *The American Republic: Primary Sources*, ed. Bruce Frohnen. Indianapolis: Liberty Fund, 2002. https://oll.libertyfund.org/page/1787-brutus-letter-i -pamphlet.

Alexander Hamilton, et al. "The Union as a Safeguard against Domestic Faction and Insurrection." In *The Federalist Papers*, ed. Clinton Rossiter. New York: Signet Classics, 2003.

Brutus. "Essay II." November 1, 1787. In *Liberty and Order: The First American Party Struggle*, ed. Lance Banning. Indianapolis: Liberty Fund, 2004. https://oll.libertyfund.org/page/1787 -brutus-essay-ii-pamphlet.

Alexander Hamilton, et al. "Certain General and Miscellaneous Objections to the Constitution Considered and Answered." In *The Federalist Papers*.

"The Convention of Virginia." June 18, 1788. In *The Debates in the Several State Conventions, vol. 3*, ed. Jonathan Elliot, 496–97. Washington: Printed by and for the editor, 1836. https://oll.libertyfund.org/title/elliot-the-debates-in-the-several-state-conventions-vol-3.

Alexander Hamilton, et al. "The Real Character of the Executive." In *The Federalist Papers*.

PART III

"The Bank Bill, [2 February] 1791." Speech by James Madison. *Founders Online*, National Archives. https://founders.archives.gov/documents/Madison/01-13-02-0282.

Thomas Jefferson. "Jefferson's Opinion on the Constitutionality of a National Bank, 1791." In *The Federalist: A Commentary on the Constitution of the United States*, by Alexander Hamilton, James Madison, and John Jay, ed. Paul Leicester Ford. New York: Henry Holt and Company, 1898.

Alexander Hamilton. "Hamilton's Opinion as to the Constitutionality of the Bank of the United States, 1791." In *The Federalist: A Commentary*.

George Washington, "Neutrality Proclamation, 22 April 1793." *Founders Online*, National Archives. https://founders.archives.gov/documents/Washington/05-12-02-0371.

Alexander Hamilton and James Madison. *The Pacificus-Helvidius Debates of 1793–1794: Toward the Completion of the American Founding*, ed. Morton J. Frisch. Indianapolis: Liberty Fund, 2007. https://oll.libertyfund.org/title/frisch-the-pacificus-helvidius-debates-of-1793-1794.

PART IV

John Adams. "May 16, 1797: Special Session Message to Congress (XYZ Affair)" (speech). Miller Center. https://millercenter.org/the-presidency/presidential-speeches/may-16-1797-special-session-message-congress-xyz-affair.

Alexander Hamilton. "Letter from Alexander Hamilton, Concerning the Public Conduct and Character of John Adams, Esq. President of the United States, [24 October 1800]." *Founders Online*, National Archives. https://founders.archives.gov/documents/Hamilton/01-25-02-0110-0002.

Alexander Hamilton to Aaron Burr. June 20, 1804, New York. *Founders Online*, National Archives. https://founders.archives.gov/documents/Hamilton/01-26-02-0001-0205.

Aaron Burr to Alexander Hamilton. June 22, 1804, New York. *Founders Online*, National Archives. https://founders.archives.gov/documents/Hamilton/01-26-02-0001-0212.

Alexander Hamilton. "Statement on Impending Duel with Aaron Burr." June 28–July 10, 1804. *Founders Online*, National Archives. https://founders.archives.gov/documents/Hamilton/01-26-02-0001-0241.

Ⓟ PENGUIN CLASSICS

Ready to find your next great read? Let us help. Visit prh.com/nextread